A Tramper's

GUIDE

to National Parks

SOUTH ISLAND 1

Robbie Burton and Maggie Atkinson

REED

To our parents

Published by Reed Books, a division of Reed Publishing (NZ) Ltd, 39 Rawene Rd, Birkenhead, Auckland. Associated companies, branches and representatives throughout the world.

Established in 1907, Reed Publishing (NZ) Ltd is New Zealand's largest book publisher, with over 300 titles in print.

For details on all these books visit our website:
www.reed.co.nz

ISBN 0 7900 0769 X

© 1987, 2001 Robbie Burton and Maggie Atkinson

The authors assert their moral rights in the work.

Cover designed by Sunny H. Yang
Text designed by Michele Stutton
Maps by Jonette Surridge

First published 1987 as *A Tramper's Guide to New Zealand's National Parks*
This edition 2001

Printed in New Zealand

contents

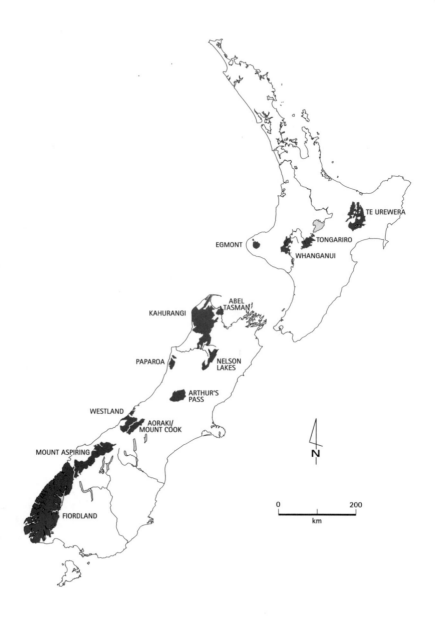

TE UREWERA

TONGARIRO
EGMONT
WHANGANUI

ABEL
TASMAN
KAHURANGI

PAPAROA
NELSON
LAKES

ARTHUR'S
PASS

WESTLAND
AORAKI/
MOUNT COOK

MOUNT ASPIRING

FIORDLAND

N

0   200
km

acknowledge*ments*

Firstly our thanks go to Mike Bradstock whose encouragement inspired the first edition of this book by Reed Methuen and sustained us to its completion. We also have appreciated the support of Ian Watt and Peter Janssen from Reed, who guided us through the most recent revision.

We remain especially grateful to Department of Conservation staff, too numerous to mention, from all our national parks, who have again checked out material and provided essential comment.

Initial research and writing for the new chapter in this edition covering Kahurangi National Park was ably undertaken, as always, by David Chowdhury.

Further support was generously provided by Joyce and Tom Atkinson, Molly Moore, Ian and Anne Miller, Derek Shaw, Andy Dennis and Bruce Thomas. We also thank Molly for her valued help with the manuscript.

Finally we would like to thank the many friends with whom we have journeyed in our national parks and who have contributed so much to our experience of these inspiring places: in particular, Peter Burton, Craig Potton, Kevin Burgess, Christine Hunt and Geoff Walls.

using this *guidebook*

Introduction and information

This book covers five of the South Island's national parks with an individual chapter. Each chapter begins with a brief introduction which is followed by a general information section. Refer to this section for details on national park visitor centres, visitor information, access, transport, services, accommodation, maps, weather and further reading.

Short walks

Most recognised walks of up to a day's duration are briefly described in the short walk section of every chapter. However, it is often difficult to distinguish between day walks and sections of longer tramps, and it is wise to consult the tramping track and route guides later in the chapter for further short walk suggestions. Each short walk is listed with the approximate time taken to complete the walk, and it is stated whether this is for a return trip by the same track, a round trip on a loop track, or a one-way trip. These times are approximate — it is essential to allow for significant variations when setting out on a walk. The grading system detailed below indicates the condition of each track and is used for all tracks and routes in this guidebook. If a short walk ventures into alpine areas allowances must be made for seasonal variations and bad weather, and a record of your intentions must be left with Department of Conservation (DOC) staff. Always carry adequate clothing and food.

Tramping

The tramping sections in each chapter all begin with a summary of most of the recognised tramping trips in that park, listed to aid the planning of a suitable trip. Following the summary are the tramping track and route guides, all broken into sections of up to a day's walking and each presenting the same standard information.

ALTITUDE

Altitude is given for the starting and finishing point of each section, as well as for any major ascent or descent. This is an important indication of the difficulty of the tramping — obviously steep climbs require more energy and time. Generally, as a very rough guide only, an average tramping party takes about an hour to climb 300 m and about half an hour to descend 300 m.

TIME

The times given for each section are approximate only. There are too many factors that influence the speed of a party (ie large parties are slower than smaller ones, fitness, weather conditions) for times to be consistently accurate. Use these times as an estimate only and allow for significant variations when planning a trip.

TRACKS AND ROUTES

Within our national parks there is great variety in the standard of paths that trampers use. The term 'track' refers to a path that has been at least cut, often formed, and marked in some way. In forest this can be by orange plastic triangles, red and white metal slats (made of permolat), round orange discs, or occasionally by blazes cut into the sides of tree trunks. In open areas wooden poles or metal standards are used, as well as cairns, small piles of rocks stacked in a rough pyramid. The term 'route' is used primarily to describe a path which is not cut or formed and often not marked at all. It is also used in a general sense when referring to the direction of travel.

GRADING SYSTEM

All tracks and routes in this guidebook, both short and long, are graded according to their condition. This is judged according to the nature of the track surface, gradient, clarity of track or route, and the presence or absence of bridges. This grading system is intended to give only *one* indication of the likely difficulty of a trip and must be considered alongside other factors, such as the ascents or descents encountered. The grades are:

Grade 1: A well-formed, benched and graded track that is easy to follow, with bridges over all major streams and rivers; or an unmarked but clear and easy route such as along a beach. Grade 1 applies to many short nature walks as well as many of New Zealand's tourist tracks, suitable for the widest range of people.

Grade 2: A marked, cut and partly formed track that is mostly easy to follow, with bridges only where necessary and often not at all. The standard New Zealand backcountry tramping track, often rough in places and requiring some tramping experience, is a typical Grade 2 track.

Grade 3: A marked, cairned, poled or obvious route with little or no formed or cut track. Typical Grade 3 routes would include a poled route across an alpine pass, an untracked route in the bush marked by artificial blazes, or a route following a streambed. Such routes require reasonably advanced bushcraft and route-finding skills.

Grade 4: An unmarked route with no track, markers, poles or cairns. Unmarked routes that cross alpine passes are typical of such a grading. A Grade 4 route often requires advanced route-finding skills and is suitable only for experienced trampers.

MAPS

The brief tramping track and route guides in this guidebook are designed to be used with topographical maps, and it is essential that maps are always carried. Consult maps regularly when tramping and learn to read them. In more difficult country carry and know how to use a compass. Details of the relevant maps for each national park are in the information section at the beginning of each chapter. Terralink NZ Ltd produce and sell maps in New Zealand, available from Department of Conservation outlets and other retail stores around the country.

TRUE LEFT AND RIGHT

The terms 'true left' and 'true right' are a standard language used by trampers to avoid confusion when talking about the different sides of a river or stream. The true left or right of a river is established by *looking downstream.*

SHELTER

One of the stamps of the national park system in New Zealand is the extensive network of huts in each park. They range from large multi-room huts to small rudimentary bivvies with two bunks and no facilities. The basic information about each hut is given in brackets in the track and route guides. The abbreviations indicate the authority in control of the hut, in most cases the relevant national park. In some instances clubs operate huts in national parks, and outside park boundaries they are normally owned by the Department of Conservation. The number of bunks is listed, as well as the cooking or heating facility present in the hut. As the forest around many huts is becoming depleted of firewood, and there may not be any cooking facility at all, cooking stoves should be carried. Most backcountry huts in national parks operate on a 'first come, first served' basis, with no booking, though the Milford and Routeburn tracks provide notable exceptions to this. During holiday periods huts are often full and at these times it is wise to carry a tent. There is a fee for staying overnight in most of these huts. The way in which hut fees are collected varies between national parks, so it is important you clarify how to pay these fees before you enter each park. The most common collection method is through tickets purchased in advance at Department of Conservation offices and other selected outlets, which are then deposited in each hut used. An Annual Hut Pass, for use in certain categories of huts, can also be used, while some parks use a Facility Use Pass for both huts and camping areas, or collect fees through hut wardens or at visitor centres. Hut fees are used to maintain the hut system in each park. Their increase in cost over recent years has been the result of budget restrictions forced on DOC by the Government. When using national park huts remember to:

- record your progress and intentions in the hut book;
- if there is a wood stove or open fire always leave a supply of dry kindling and firewood;
- if fuel is provided (ie wood, coal, gas) use it sparingly;
- ensure the hut is dry, clean and tidy while there and before leaving;
- to prevent rusting, leave all billies, pans and buckets clean and upside down;
- ensure that fireplaces and stoves are swept and clean before leaving;
- check that all windows and doors are securely shut before leaving.

In some national parks there are rock bivvies which can be used, normally overhanging boulders or cliffs that provide shelter from the weather, and are often quite comfortable and characterful.

TRACK CHANGES

It is important when using these guides always to allow for the possibility of seasonal, natural and artificial changes to tracks and routes. Many become difficult, dangerous or impassable when under snow. If the guide states that alpine experience and equipment are necessary this means that ice axe, crampons and rope should be carried, and that trampers should have the experience and skill to use them. Flooding, common in New Zealand, often makes many tracks and routes temporarily difficult or impassable. It also causes washouts, landslides and the destruction of bridges, and along with windthrow and avalanche damage can create drastic changes to backcountry tracks and routes. Upgrading and modification of tracks, bridges and huts are ongoing in national parks and this should always be remembered when tramping.

GIARDIA

Giardia is a parasite that can live in the human intestine and cause severe diarrhoea. It is unfortunately found in some lakes, rivers and streams in New Zealand's national parks. You should be aware of how to avoid spreading the parasite, and familiar with the techniques of purifying water that may be contaminated with giardia, by either boiling the water for more than three minutes, or using portable filtering mechanisms or chemical purification.

Tramping in a national park

All those who use our national parks should never forget the inestimable value of these splendid and inspiring areas. Every tramper has a personal responsibility to respect and support the ethic of preservation that underlies our national park system. To keep the impact of your presence to a minimum and to adhere to national park regulations, remember this environmental code:

- protect plants and animals — they are unique and often rare;
- remove rubbish — carry out what you carry in;
- bury toilet waste if there are no toilets;
- keep streams and lakes clean — do your cleaning and washing away from them;
- use portable fuel stoves whenever you can — if you must use wood fires keep them small, use only dead wood and take care to extinguish them after use;
- camp carefully — leave no trace of your visit;
- keep to the track to avoid damaging fragile plants;
- be considerate of others when you visit the backcountry;
- respect our cultural heritage when visiting places that have spiritual or historical significance;
- enjoy your outdoor experience — protect the environment for your own sake, for the sake of those who come after you, and for the environment itself.

All national parks have at least one area office and visitor centre, where up-to-date information, interpretive displays, tramping advice, maps, publications, weather forecasts, and firearm and hunting permits are usually available, and hut fees can be paid. Free rubbish bags, in which you can carry your rubbish out of the national park, are available from some visitor centres.

This is also where clear records of your tramping intentions can often be left before beginning your trip, in which case you *must* check out when your trip is safely completed. Failure to do this may result in an expensive and unnecessary search and rescue operation. It should be noted, though, that systems for leaving tramping intentions vary between parks (some require you to leave tramping intentions with a relative or friend) and this should be checked with each national park. In the event of an emergency, contact Department of Conservation staff as soon as possible.

All national parks run summer and holiday programmes for park visitors. They are an excellent way of learning more about the park, and usually consist of guided walks and other outdoor activities, talks and slide or film shows. Details of these programmes can be obtained from park visitor centres.

useful information
for trampers

This chapter contains some basic advice that may make a tramping trip into a national park more enjoyable, comfortable and safe. For more detailed information the comprehensive and practical mountain safety manual *Bushcraft* (New Zealand Mountain Safety Council) is an excellent place to begin. Remember, however, that no amount of reading or advice can replace first-hand experience. If you are new to tramping, begin by tackling the easier and more popular tracks, and save the more difficult routes until you have developed more experience.

What to take

The careful selection of clothing, equipment and food is an essential prerequisite to a successful tramp. Take time and trouble over this and carry only what you need — nothing more and nothing less. A light pack can add considerably to the enjoyment of a trip.

CLOTHING
Footwear
If you intend to travel in rough or alpine terrain, a strong pair of leather or plastic boots is necessary. They must be comfortable, provide good support and be durable, and should be 'worn in' before setting out. Lace-up rubber gumboots are suitable in a lot of tramping country, and on easy tracks lightweight boots or running shoes can be adequate. Always carry a spare pair of bootlaces. Knee-high wool, or wool/synthetic-mix, socks are best; carry enough pairs to always have a dry change. Gaiters or puttees to keep water, snow, mud and other debris out of your boots are a popular and useful piece of equipment. If weight is not critical, a lightweight pair of shoes (ie running

shoes) or sport sandals is useful around huts or campsites, and can also provide a back-up for uncomfortable boots.

Tramping clothes

Depending on the season and the area, clothing requirements will change, though the basics stay the same. Carry a change of underwear. Many trampers favour a light cotton shirt for comfort next to the skin. One or two polypropylene or woollen singlets (long-sleeved are preferable in cold or wet conditions) should be carried, along with a fleece or woollen shirt or light jersey. As a final layer a fleece jacket or heavier woollen bush shirt or jersey is essential. Shorts (handy if they have pockets) should always be carried, along with fleece or woollen trousers and/or one or two pairs of polypropylene or woollen long johns worn under shorts. It is important to plan your clothing combinations so that you are always able to keep, in a plastic bag, some dry clothes that can be worn next to your skin when you reach shelter. Because it is warm when wet or dry, wool was always the traditional material favoured by trampers, but has generally been surpassed by the synthetic fleeces and polypropylene, which are not only warm when wet or dry, but absorb far less water than wool and consequently dry much faster.

For cold weather a balaclava or hat, and mittens or gloves, are essential — a lot of heat is lost through the head, and on a cold night in a sleeping bag a balaclava or hat can make a great difference. In sunny weather a sunhat can be valuable, and if you wear glasses a peaked rainhat is very useful in the rain. Always carry a handkerchief: good for sweaty brows as well as for picking up hot billies! Don't forget your sunglasses.

Rain and wind protection

Effective rain and wind protection is a vital part of any tramper's wardrobe. A sturdy, roomy parka of a breathable laminated fabric is best. Light wind-breakers or padded jackets are not adequate. Even with the laminated fabrics that breathe, condensation and perspiration usually build up underneath a parka when tramping in the rain. This often means getting wet, despite your protection, and you should always allow for this. Overtrousers should be carried to cut out wind and some rain, especially if travelling in alpine areas. Lightweight overtrousers are usually adequate, and are more practical if they have zips up the side so that they can easily be pulled on over boots.

EQUIPMENT

Packs

Tramping packs are built with either internal or external frames. Internal frame packs are generally more comfortable and easier to walk with, while the more traditional external frame packs do allow better ventilation. Whatever your choice look for something comfortable built of strong, waterproof and tough material. Avoid excessive numbers of zips, fittings and adjusters. They often serve little purpose but to provide something more that can break on your pack. No pack is completely waterproof so pack everything in plastic bags. A large plastic pack liner is useful as well.

Sleeping

Cold, sleepless nights don't make for good tramping so choose a sleeping bag carefully. Down is the warmest, lightest and most expensive filling for a bag. It is useless when wet, however, though breathable and waterproof fabrics now used as the outer covering on some sleeping bags help prevent this. Synthetic fillings for sleeping bags are reasonably warm and retain some warmth when wet, though are more bulky than down. With warm sleeping bags a long zip is preferable to avoid overheating in summer. If sleeping outside (or on hut floors) a self-inflating or closed-cell foam sleeping mat is an excellent companion, providing comfort and good insulation as well as keeping the damp out. A waterproof groundsheet will keep a bag dry and provide shelter in an emergency.

Shelter

In either remote or crowded parts of our national parks, tents or flysheets are essential. Good tents are expensive but worth it. Many of our national parks have a high rainfall and it is essential that tents be waterproof, which usually means they will have two skins and be adequately ventilated to prevent condensation. They need to be light, and it is an advantage if they have their own poles, a built-in floor and insect netting. Instead of a tent, a nylon flysheet and groundsheet can be used on their own as a pleasant option in summer.

Cooking, eating and drinking

Carrying a cooking stove is not only ecologically sound, but also convenient and fast, especially in bad weather. A good stove should be efficient (fuelled by either white spirits, kerosene or gas), reasonably light and strong enough to take a battering in your pack. Learn how to safely operate your stove, carry fuel with care, and on longer trips carry spare parts. If you are relying on fires, make sure matches are kept dry and have back-up firelighting aids such as candles or solid-fuel tablets. Axes and saws for chopping wood are generally not necessary.

For cooking take aluminium billies with fitting lids and carry them packed with food inside your pack. It is worth making or buying a cloth or nylon stuff-bag for billies to keep their soot off the contents of your pack. A pot cleaner and tea towel are useful and light additions. If travelling in country where water is scarce, carry a water container. A deep plastic bowl is far more useful than a shallow plate for eating, and take a large light mug — you tend to drink a lot of liquid when tramping. A spoon is sufficient for eating. Carry a small sharp knife — large heavy knives are not necessary.

First aid

A comprehensive first aid kit must be carried within each party. Consult *Outdoor First Aid* (New Zealand Mountain Safety Council) for a suggested kit. It is also convenient for individuals to carry a small personal kit with commonly used things such as sticking plaster and sunscreen. Don't forget insect repellent.

Essential extras

A small torch (carried with a battery reversed to stop it accidentally switching on) is necessary within each party, and normally so are candles. Map and compass are critical, and a small survival kit is wise. Personal toilet gear and a towel shouldn't be forgotten, and it is useful to carry spare plastic bags (the more durable rubbish bags are good). A little repair kit with such things as cord, needle, thread, and thin wire is handy on longer trips. Someone in the party should carry a waterproof watch — one with an alarm is useful for early starts. If you are planning on a relaxed tramp don't forget a good book (not hardback!) or magazine.

FOOD FOR TRAMPING

Food can contribute greatly to the enjoyment of a tramping trip, but can just as easily detract. It is worth taking care to ensure that tramping food is nourishing, sustaining and enjoyable to all in the party. When choosing tramping food:

- look for a combination of high food value and low weight;
- aim for simplicity in cooking — 'one pot' meals that require the minimum of cooking are the most convenient;
- don't take tinned food or anything in jars — it is heavy and you would be carrying unnecessary rubbish into the bush;
- choose food that keeps well;
- avoid foods likely to be damaged when carried and jostled in a pack, or that are excessively bulky.

The final selection of a tramping menu will have much to do with the length of the planned trip. On an overnight trip where extra weight is not too important, few concessions have to be made and all manner of foods can be taken. However, when a trip gets longer than three to four days the sustenance provided and the weight and the life of the food carried become much more important. Generally a dry weight of around 1 kg per person per day is sufficient for most people, but this can be reduced as low as 750 g per person per day when weight is critical and the party prepared to accept a very limited diet.

Breakfast should be substantial — breakfast cereals, such as muesli, are obviously most common, while others prefer something hot, such as porridge. It is often, however, a real advantage to avoid cooking in the mornings, as it saves both time and fuel. It is wise to follow a first course based on carbohydrates (such as muesli) with some food containing fats, which could include such things as bread with butter and a spread like peanut butter. Have a large hot drink with breakfast as it helps to counter dehydration later in the day.

A lunch of bread or crackers with a variety of spreads and toppings is widely accepted among trampers. Apart from being better for you, wholegrain breads stay fresh longer and stand up to more punishment in a pack. As well, choose crackers that will not disintegrate when carried in a pack. On longer trips margarine will last longer than butter, and processed cheese will last longer than standard cheese. If you have the time and the fuel, a 'brew' at lunch is often a welcome treat. When weight is not a problem many other luxuries can be included for lunch, such as fruit or sweet biscuits.

For convenience, many trampers carry prepared, freeze-dried or instant dinners for their evening meal, which have substantially improved in recent years. When choosing them ensure that they are reasonably easy to prepare and remember that many people require larger servings than the packets allow for. They are also often improved by adding extra ingredients of your choice, such as vegetables or meat. A usually cheaper and more flexible alternative to instant meals is to carry suitable ingredients to prepare your own dinner, most commonly based on rice or pasta, to which a combination of other ingredients and flavourings are added, such as dehydrated and fresh vegetables, meat, sauces, cheese and spices. These kinds of meals can be greatly enhanced by careful use of spices, herbs and other condiments. If you are taking your own rice or pasta you generally need around 100–125 g per person. Remember to take salt. With desserts, allow for extra ingredients such as milk powder. Many trampers don't bother to prepare desserts and simply take something sweet to have with a hot drink after dinner.

Snack food during the day is an important source of energy when walking.

Scroggin is the name given to a mixture of chocolate, nuts, dried fruit and sweets that has become the standard snack for New Zealand trampers, though there are no end of alternatives to scroggin now available, including the many varieties of fruit and nut based snack bars.

It is important to drink plenty of liquid when tramping to replace fluid lost through sweating, so remember to take generous amounts of drinks, both hot and cold.

Packing

Pack and protect carefully the food you take tramping. Use double plastic bags tied off with twisties or rubber bands to keep the contents in and water out. Small plastic containers can be useful for many items, especially spreads such as jam and honey. On longer trips it is advisable to divide and pack food into measured meal or day portions to allow easy rationing.

TRAMPING SAFELY

Preparation

Safe tramping begins with thorough preparation. To collect information about your route, use this guidebook, maps and the knowledge of people who know the area you intend visiting. Try to match your experience, fitness and the time of year with an appropriate tramp. Ensure that the tramp selected is suitable for all members of the party, and don't tramp alone unless very experienced. Always leave clear intentions of where you are going with national park staff, or with other responsible people.

Reaching your destination

Getting an early start when tramping is a very sensible thing to do. Not only is early morning a pleasant time for walking, but it is far wiser to have any available spare time at the end of the day rather than wasting it in the morning. Should anything unforeseen delay progress, any extra hours of daylight gained by starting early may make the difference between reaching your destination and having an unplanned night out. Once walking, set a pace that is suitable for all members of your party. Try to keep your pace steady and at a speed that is sustainable all day. Remember to always keep together, and never leave slower members of your party behind.

Developing the skill to stay on a track or route is obviously critical to getting where you want to go, and one of the keys to this is learning to be observant. Keep looking both ahead and behind to stay on route and be aware of the landmarks around you to ensure a general orientation. Regularly trace your progress on a map even if you don't need to, as it all adds to your sense of direction. If you stray off the track or route, immediately retrace your steps until you find it again, and don't plough on in the hope you will eventually regain it. Make sure you carry a compass, and that you know how to use it. Should it become apparent that you are not going to make your destination that day, stop well before dark so that you have enough light to set up camp or find shelter.

Weather

The weather has an enormous influence on tramping, and having an understanding of weather patterns and their effect is a valuable skill for a tramper. The weather in New Zealand's backcountry is notoriously unpredictable and fast to change. Learn to read and consult weather maps, and get up-to-date weather forecasts before setting out. Develop your awareness of the weather and by observation and experience learn to recognise weather signs. Most bad weather is preceded by tell-tale signs, and spotting these may enable you to avoid a potentially dangerous situation.

Above the bushline

Many national park tramping tracks and routes lead into alpine areas above the bushline. These can often be the most spectacular and exciting parts of a tramp but also the most dangerous. The weather is likely to be far more severe than at lower altitudes, with colder temperatures, stronger winds and heavier snow and rain. Don't venture above the bushline in bad weather or poor visibility, and in fine weather always carry adequate equipment should you get caught in a weather change. Beware of snow slopes which can become icy and highly dangerous at all times of the year. Avoid traversing above bluffs and remember that wet snowgrass is very slippery.

Rivers

Crossing rivers is one of the greatest hazards of tramping in New Zealand and the cause of many fatal accidents. Never take a river crossing lightly. Learn the techniques of mutual support for river crossing and how to assess the safest place to cross. Never cross swollen or discoloured rivers unless completely sure that the ford is safe. Although rivers often rise very quickly in rain, they go down just as rapidly and it is far safer to wait for a river to drop than to risk your life attempting a crossing. Even with experience it is wise to always be extremely cautious.

First aid

Everyone venturing into the backcountry should have a basic understanding of first aid. A very good starting point is *Outdoor First Aid* (New Zealand Mountain Safety Council), which outlines the basic information that trampers should know. A common hazard in the outdoors is hypothermia (or exposure), which occurs when a person's body temperature drops below normal. This potentially fatal situation is often caused by cold, wet or windy conditions. Learn how to prevent hypothermia, what its signs are, and what to do if you suspect someone has it. In the event of a serious injury or illness within your party, or a missing person, it may be necessary to seek help. If possible, leave one person to look after the injured person and send two people out. It is important that those going for help take a written message that contains the following information:

- what has happened, with details of what assistance is required;
- who is involved, with details of names, ages, experience and addresses of all people involved, the physical and mental condition of all involved and as much detail as possible on the injuries or illness and treatment given. A list of gear they have, and the name and address of the party's contact person (if there is one) and next of kin are also important.
- where they are, with a clear description of the exact location of the party, and where a missing person was last seen, the weather, river and snow conditions in the area, as well as the travelling time from the road end.

This information will be of real value to those organising a search and rescue operation.

Survival

No matter how well prepared you are there is always the possibility that you will have to cope with a survival situation, and it is essential to be familiar with basic survival techniques. Some things to remember are:

- always carry either a small survival kit, or the essential items of a kit, such as some kind of emergency shelter and firelighting equipment. It is also wise to include such things as a whistle, cord, sharp knife, fish hooks and line, and pencil and paper.
- when finding yourself in a survival situation, stop, stay calm, carefully assess your situation and plan what you are going to do;
- keep warm by finding, improvising or building shelter, using what clothing you have to keep dry and warm, and lighting a fire if possible. Improvise with whatever you have to make extra clothing.
- it is important to drink plenty of water. Ration your foods as well, but don't spend excessive energy trying to catch or gather extra food.
- do whatever you can to help searchers find you. Use such things as a smoky fire, brightly coloured objects or cairns to attract attention.

abel tasman *national park*

At the northern end of the South Island, Abel Tasman National Park encompasses an area of coastline and hill country curling up the western side of Tasman Bay and around into Golden Bay. Formed in 1942, it is by New Zealand standards a small national park. It is best known for its coastline, a tranquil, almost exotic complex of bays, headlands, islands, reefs, lagoons and sparkling beaches, while also including a block of rugged hills rising back from the sea to a height of just over 1130 m.

The park principally sits astride a huge dome of granite, which over many millions of years has tilted to now lie lower in the east than the west. This granite has the characteristic of weathering at a variety of speeds, so the streams flowing down to the coast have carved jumbled gorges in the sections of weaker granite. Wave action has eroded the bays on the coast out of the softer rock, leaving them divided by headlands and dotted with islands and reefs of granite more resistant to erosion. On a smaller scale this weathering process is reflected in the sculptural shapes found everywhere in the Abel Tasman rock.

Though the park's landforms have changed little since the arrival of Europeans this has sadly not been the case with the vegetation. Once, this corner of Tasman Bay was covered in forest. On the moist, warmer sites lush rainforest grew, and on the drier ridges and in the cooler upland areas species of beech tree filled out the forest canopy. But now a century of fire and milling has left around three-quarters of the country along the coast significantly modified and the original forest standing only in remnant patches. In place of this forest is a mixture of introduced shrubs and trees, and regenerating native vegetation. The park's guardians have an enormous job in encouraging and overseeing the slow process of healing.

Despite the damage that has been done the park still has a rich, natural world. Birdlife abounds in the forests, shrublands and on the quiet estuaries and beaches, and there is endless scope for exploring and enjoying the marine world on the coastline.

Abel Tasman National Park would seem to have been an idyllic place to live, with its sheltered bays and settled weather. Surprisingly it has never supported a large population. Though Maori had settlements dotted up the coastline, these were never big, and evidence suggests it was a reasonable struggle to survive.

The Dutch navigator Abel Tasman was the first European to discover New Zealand, and also the first to encounter what is now the park. His two ships spent a night at anchor, most likely off Whariwharangi Beach, before leaving the next day after a skirmish with the local Maori people. The first real European exploration of the park came with the visit of Frenchman Dumont D'Urville and the crew of his corvette *Astrolabe* in 1827. They spent a relaxed week in what is now Astrolabe Roadstead, enjoying the delightful environment and positive contact with local Maori.

As the Nelson region was settled, people inevitably came to make their homes on this coastline. The tall coastal forest attracted sawmillers and boatbuilders, and pockets of flat land supported farmers and their families. However, the timber did not last, the impoverished granite soils made farming a struggle and the population never flourished. Things have not changed, and virtually all people in the park now are itinerant — those who come for holidays in baches built on pockets of private land along the coast, campers at Totaranui, sea kayakers on the coast, and the thousands of walkers who come to enjoy the tracks in this park.

The flavour of tramping in Abel Tasman is best described as relaxed. The tracks following the coast are gentle and well formed, the distance between huts and camping areas short, and the weather sunnier and milder than in any other national park in New Zealand. The tracks climbing up into the interior are also within reach of all average trampers. The diversions for the walker are numerous: beautiful beaches for sunbathing and swimming, large sandy estuaries to explore, many side-walks, a smattering of historic relics and long stretches of rocky coastline on which to fossick. This combination encourages a tramping holiday of a style unique in our national parks, and one that is accessible to the widest range of people.

Information

PARK VISITOR CENTRES AND AREA OFFICES
The northern and Canaan end of the park is administered from the DOC office in Commercial Street, Takaka. The address for enquiries is:

> Golden Bay Area Office
> Department of Conservation
> PO Box 166

62 Commercial Street
Takaka
Phone (03) 525 8026
Fax (03) 525 8444

The southern end of the park from Tonga to Marahau is administered from the DOC office in High Street, Motueka. The address for enquiries is:

Motueka Area Office
Department of Conservation
PO Box 97
Motueka
Phone (03) 528 1810
Fax (03) 528 1811

There is a DOC staff-member based at Totaranui (ph (03) 528 8083) where there is an office and visitor centre, open daily during the summer months. There are intentions books at both ends of the Coast Track at Marahau and Wainui, at Totaranui, Pages Saddle at Canaan and Bird's Clearing near Takaka.

ACCESS

The Marahau end of the park can be reached by the Coastal Road through Kaiteriteri, and the Riwaka–Sandy Bay Road, both of which branch off SH 60 past Riwaka. The Canaan entrance to the park is reached on a rough road which branches off SH 60 on top of Takaka Hill on the Nelson side of the summit. Totaranui is reached from Takaka on the road to Tarakohe which leads onto the Totaranui Road. Branching off the Totaranui Road behind Wainui Bay, McShanes Road gives access to the start of the Coast Track, and a winding road off the Totaranui Road south of Awaroa Saddle leads down to Awaroa Inlet. Most of the coastline in the park is easily accessible from the sea.

TRANSPORT SERVICES

The Nelson Visitor Information Centre (phone (03) 548 2304) takes bookings for the major operators who provide transport to or near the park. These include the Abel Tasman Coachlines (phone (03) 548 1539) who run a bus service between Nelson, Motueka and Marahau; Abel Tasman National Park Enterprises (phone (03) 528 7801) whose launch service up the coast and connecting bus service to Nelson, Motueka and Golden Bay is used extensively by trampers; and Golden Bay Book-A-Bus who provide connections to the Golden Bay end of the Park. There are a number of other operators providing boat transport into the park, including Abel Tasman

Seafaris (phone (03) 527 8083), Water-Taxi Charter at Kaiteriteri (phone (025) 425 401) and the Spirit of Golden Bay which operates between Tarakohe in Golden Bay and Nelson (phone (03) 525 9135). Another more exciting method of transport within the park is to hire your own sea kayak from the Ocean River Adventure Company (phone (03) 528 8823) or Abel Tasman Kayaks (phone (03) 527 8022).

ACCOMMODATION

Camping areas: The park has campsites with toilets and water at Whariwharangi, Mutton Cove, Anapai, Awaroa Hut, Onetahuti, Tonga Quarry, Bark Bay, Torrent Bay (west of settlement), Anchorage Hut, Te Pukatea Bay, Watering Cove, Observation Beach, Appletree Bay, Tinline and the Canaan Road end.

Camping grounds: There is a camping ground operated by the park at Totaranui. Bookings are necessary between 1 December and 31 January and can be made on the park's application form after 1 July every year. There are motor camps outside the park at Marahau, Kaiteriteri and Pohara.

Motels, hotels and lodges: There are motels and hotels at Motueka, Takaka and Riwaka, and motels at Kaiteriteri, Pohara, Tata Beach and Takaka, and a lodge at Awaroa.

SERVICES

Both Takaka and Motueka have all the services normally found in a small town. The closest shops at the southern end of the park are at Kaiteriteri and Riwaka, as well as a shop selling food for trampers at Marahau. During the summer months the visitor centre at Totaranui sells a small range of food, drink and other useful items, while the cafe at the Awaroa Lodge sells food and other useful items.

WEATHER

Abel Tasman National Park boasts an extremely favourable climate, the best of any national park in New Zealand. Sunshine hours are high, summers hot and winters reasonably mild. On the coast the park receives about 1800 mm of rain a year, with no obvious wet season. In the upland areas the climate is colder and wetter than that on the coast, with occasional snowfalls during winter. The gentle climate of Abel Tasman poses little problem to the tramper, and makes it an ideal place for trips in winter as well as summer.

MAPS

Parkmap 273/07 of Abel Tasman National Park covers the entire park, and has all huts and tracks marked. Alternatively trampers can use the Topomap 260 series, N26 Takaka and N25 Tarakohe.

FURTHER READING

The park handbook *A Park for All Seasons: the Story of Abel Tasman National Park* (Abel Tasman National Park, 1985) gives the best insight into the natural and social history and the recreational values of the park. The park authorities have also published numerous interesting booklets and pamphlets on a variety of natural and historical subjects.

Short walks

WALKS FROM THE TOTARANUI ROAD

Wainui Falls: 1 hour return, Grade 1.
A short road leads off the Totaranui Road behind Wainui Bay to the beginning of a track up to Wainui Falls. This picturesque waterfall is on the lower reaches of the broken Wainui River.

Taupo Point: 2 hours return, Grade 1.
On the Totaranui Road before it leaves the hinterland of Wainui, McShanes Road turns off and leads to the carpark at the beginning of the Coast Track. Follow the track for a few minutes before dropping down a short side-track to the edge of the estuary. Here easy walking along the shoreline leads to Taupo Point, an old Maori pa site. On the neck of land that connects Taupo Point with the mainland there is a pleasant grassy area suitable for picnicking or camping, with a reliable water supply. This is not accessible at high tide.

Lookout Rock: 1 hour return, Grade 1.
At Pigeon Saddle, the highest point on the winding road between Wainui and Totaranui, a track leads off to Lookout Rock through forest dotted with large beech and podocarp trees. The rock gives good views over the surrounding hills and coastline.

WALKS AROUND TOTARANUI

The following walks all begin from the carpark at the end of the road that leads north past the Education Centre behind Totaranui Beach.

Headlands Track: 1 hour return, Grade 1.
Begin by following the Pukatea Walk to a junction where the Headlands Track branches off opposite the boat ramp. It then climbs up through forest onto the headland ridge, giving good views through the bush to the sequence of bays

and headlands to the south. The track then works back past Anapai Bay and back to the carpark.

Pukatea Walk: 30 minutes return, Grade 1, pamphlet available.

This loop track skirts around a coastal swamp before climbing up the hillside through a series of vegetation types. After dropping back down to the swamp you can either return to the carpark, or at low tide cross the estuary to the camping ground.

Anapai Bay Track: 1¹/₂ hours return, Grade 1.

One of the most popular around Totaranui, this track (actually part of the Coast Track — see p. 29) climbs to a low saddle and then drops gently down through a valley of lush forest to Anapai Bay. Framed by granite headlands, this sheltered bay is renowned for its beautiful beach. An alternative return trip uses the Headlands Track and the Pukatea Walk (see above) to complete a circuit.

Separation Point: 4–5 hours return, Grade 2.

Separation Point is the exposed granite headland that separates Tasman Bay from Golden Bay. It normally hosts a colony of fur seals over autumn and winter. From the carpark follow the Coast Track (see p. 29) to Anapai Bay and around the coast to Mutton Cove where the track to Separation Point splits off for a 30-minute walk along this headland.

Gibbs Hill: various times, Grade 2.

Gibbs Hill above Totaranui is accessible via five access routes from three different places. From Totaranui the track leaves part way up the Anapai Bay Track (see above). From Pigeon Saddle on the Totaranui Road the track initially follows the Lookout Rock Track and splits to continue to Gibbs Hill. From the Coast Track (see p. 29) between Wainui and Whariwharangi a track peels off to climb up Gibbs Hill. It is visited primarily for panoramic views, the track passing through dry shrubland, predominantly gorse or manuka regeneration. There is no water on the routes to Gibbs Hill.

Te Mata o te Moana: 2¹/₂ hours return, Grade 1, low tide only, pamphlet available.

Te Mata o te Moana translates as 'the edge of the sea' and describes this route which is not a track but more a nature ramble using the descriptive pamphlet to explain the natural world encountered. The route begins in the freshwater swamp off the tree-lined avenue behind Totaranui and passes through saltmarsh and sandflat to end up on the rocky shore at the northern end of Totaranui Bay.

Waiharakeke Track: 2¹/₂ hours return, Grade 2.

The Waiharakeke Track begins on the road to Awaroa, dropping down through bush to Waiharakeke Beach and the Coast Track. For much of the way the track follows the line of an old bush tramway, built to bring logs to the sawmill that once worked at Waiharakeke Beach.

WALKS AROUND TORRENT BAY

These walks are not accessible by car, but are for those with time to spare at Torrent Bay who have either walked in or arrived by boat.

Falls River Waterfall Track: 2 hours return from lagoon, Grade 2.

This track offers a good insight into the rugged hill country behind the coast, as well as a view of a major waterfall on the Falls River, and leaves the all-tides track around Torrent Bay Lagoon (see p. 30) just to the east of the settlement. It follows up Tregidga Creek passing the Cascade Falls after about 30 minutes, before dropping down to the Falls River 15 minutes downstream of the waterfalls. To reach the falls scramble upriver, crossing the river twice.

Cleopatra's Pool: 45 minutes return from Torrent Bay camping area, 1¹/₂ hours return from Anchorage Hut, Grade 2.

By following the all-tides track around Torrent Bay Lagoon (see p. 30), or by following up the Torrent River at low tide, the footbridge over the Torrent River in the lagoon's southwest corner can be reached. From here a short track leads to Cleopatra's Pool, a large 'bathtub' ground out of the granite streambed by the Torrent River.

Pitt Head and Te Pukatea Bay: 1 hour round trip, Grade 1, pamphlet available.

This track begins at the Anchorage Hut camping area, and leads out to Pitt Head, the site of an old Maori headland fortification, before dropping down to Te Pukatea Bay. With a curving, sheltered beach Te Pukatea offers campsites for those with tents. From Te Pukatea Bay follow the track up from the beach to reconnect with the Pitt Head Track and the track back to Anchorage.

Watering Cove: 1¹/₂ hours return, Grade 2.

With its golden sand, granite rocks and coastal forest creeping down to the shore, Watering Cove is a classic Abel Tasman bay. Its name commemorates the explorer D'Urville's visit to pick up water in 1827. The cove can be reached on a track that splits off the track connecting Anchorage Beach and the Coast Track. There is a campsite behind the cove.

WALKS AROUND MARAHAU

Tinline Nature Walk: 1¹/₂ hours return from Marahau carpark, Grade 1, pamphlet available.

From the Marahau carpark the rather barren beginning of the Coast Track (see p. 29) leads to the Tinline camping area. Here the Tinline Nature Walk begins, a 30-minute loop track that illustrates the contrast between the original forest cover and the country razed by fire.

Coquille Bay: 1¹/₂ hours return, Grade 1.
Coquille Bay can be reached from the Marahau carpark on the Coast Track (see p. 29). With a pleasant beach for picnicking or swimming, Coquille Bay is the next bay after the Tinline camping area, reached by a short side-track off the Coast Track.

Appletree Bay: 3 hours return, Grade 1.
As with the Coquille Bay walk this trip is primarily a walk along the Coast Track (see p. 29) from the Marahau carpark. Appletree Bay is in the stretch of water known as the Astrolabe Roadstead and is reached by a short track off the Coast Track. Just off the beach there is a camping area with a toilet and water supply.

WALKS FROM THE CANAAN ROAD END

Harwoods Hole: 1¹/₂ hours, Grade 2, pamphlet available.
Harwoods Hole is a massive shaft that drops 176 m vertically into the ancient marble of the Pikikiruna Range on the western fringe of the park. This spectacular hole is reached on a mainly gentle track through beech forest that leaves from the camping and picnic area at the end of the Canaan Road. Visitors to the Hole are warned to go no further than the viewpoint. About 10 minutes back up the track a marked side-track is worth following as it leads to an airy perch above the head of the Gorge Creek Valley, with views down into the Takaka Valley. Take care as the edge of the viewpoint drops steeply away and the jagged marble underfoot can be treacherous.

Tramping trip summary

This summary outlines most of the recognised tramping trips in Abel Tasman National Park. Used with the route descriptions that follow it can provide a basis for planning a tramp. Remember, however, that these are only suggestions and by using a map and consulting park staff many variations on these tramps can be found. The times given make no allowance for delays caused by bad weather.

- Beginning at Marahau, the Coast Track to Wainui Bay, or reversed, beginning from Wainui Bay (2¹/₂–5 days). Variation: shorten trip by either beginning or ending tramp at Totaranui or Awaroa (2¹/₂–3 days).
- Beginning at Wainui or Totaranui, the Coast Track to Torrent Bay or Tinline Bay, then inland tracks via Castle Rocks, Moa Park and Awapoto Hut to Totaranui Road (4–6 days).
- Beginning at Canaan carpark, to Moa Park and then to Marahau via Castle Rocks and Tinline Bay (2 days).

- Beginning at Canaan carpark, to Moa Park and to Totaranui Road via Awapoto Hut (2 days). Variation: continue to Whariwharangi from Pigeon Saddle via Gibbs Hill, and out to either Wainui or Totaranui via Coast (add $^1/_2$–1 day).
- Beginning at Canaan carpark, to Central Takaka in Takaka Valley via Rameka Road and the farm road ($^1/_2$–1 day).
- Beginning at Canaan carpark, to Clifton via Wainui Valley and Bird's Clearing (1 day).

Tramping

THE COAST TRACK

The Coast Track is an easy, scenic, year-round and understandably popular tramp. All major streams are bridged, but two large estuaries, one of which cannot be avoided, are on the route. DOC provides a range of accomodation along the track, including four huts, 21 campsites and the Totaranui campground. There are charges for the use of these facilities, and visitors must purchase their passes to use these facilities before starting the track. Visitors wanting to use the huts during the peak season of 1 October to 30 April must book hut space before their trip. There is a two consecutive night limit on staying in any one hut or campsite throughout the year. The track surface is good and light-weight boots or running shoes are adequate footwear. Though the following track description starts at Wainui Bay the Coast Track can just as easily be started at Marahau. If time is short it is also possible to begin or end the walk at either Totaranui or Awaroa. Note: All huts and campsites on the Coast Track are near enough to sea level so altitude is not listed in the track information.

Wainui carpark to Whariwharangi Hut: 1$^1/_2$ hours, Grade 1.
The Wainui carpark is reached from the Totaranui Road by McShanes Road behind Wainui Bay. Alternatively the carpark can be gained by leaving the Totaranui Road on the western side of the Wainui estuary and crossing the estuary on foot, safe up to 2 hours either side of low tide. From the carpark an old farm track winds over hills covered in gorse and regenerating native shrubland to Whariwharangi Bay. This area was inhabited until 1926 and farmed until 1972. The Whariwharangi Hut (DOC, 20 bunks, wood stove) is the old restored farmhouse. An alternative route to Whariwharangi is via the Gibbs Hill track (see p. 26).

Whariwharangi Hut to Totaranui: 3 hours, Grade 1.
From Whariwharangi Bay the old farm track crosses a low saddle to Mutton Cove tucked in the lee of Separation Point (for Separation Point Track see page

26). Mutton Cove has a campsite behind the beach. From Mutton Cove continue around the beach and over the headland to Anapai Bay, which also has a campsite. Here the track leaves the coast and climbs up a forested valley to a low saddle and a gentle descent to Totaranui. Walkers on the Coast Track are able to stay overnight in the Totaranui camping ground without booking.

Totaranui to Awaroa Hut: 1¹/₂–2 hours, Grade 1.

This section must be timed to allow a crossing of the Awaroa estuary. Pick up the Coast Track again at the southern end of Totaranui Beach. After skirting Skinner Point it follows around Goat Bay to Waiharakeke Bay. Here the track leaves the coast and crosses over to the edge of Awaroa Inlet where the route, marked by big discs, leads directly over the estuary to the Awaroa Hut (DOC, 26 bunks, wood stove) on the far side. This crossing is quite safe up to 2 hours either side of low tide but should not be attempted at any other time. It also becomes impassable when the Awaroa River is in flood.

Awaroa Hut to Bark Bay Hut: 3 hours, Grade 1.

The pattern of alternating bays and headlands changes past Awaroa. From the hut follow around the edge of the estuary towards the sea and the cluster of private baches. The track climbs up to the shrub-covered Tonga Saddle from behind this settlement and drops down to a large swamp behind Onetahuti (sometimes known as Big Tonga). Richardson Stream at the northern end of the beach can be difficult to cross at high tide. Continue along the beach and follow the track over to the site of the old Tonga Quarry where granite was once quarried and used for building such things as Nelson's cathedral steps. Beyond the quarry the track sticks to an easy grade before dropping through beech forest to Bark Bay. If the tide is out, this picturesque estuary is easily crossed to the Bark Bay Hut (DOC, 24 bunks, wood stove) tucked in the southwest corner. If not, there is an all-tides track around the estuary, worth walking even if the tide is out. There are many good campsites at Bark Bay.

Bark Bay Hut to Torrent Bay and Anchorage Hut: 2¹/₂–4 hours, Grade 1.

Between Bark Bay and Torrent Bay, the track crosses some of the more rugged country on the coast, much of which is still clothed in forest. South of Bark Bay a short track leads out to a viewpoint back from South Head. A little further on, a track leads down to Sandfly Bay and the mouth of the Falls River. A swingbridge spans the Falls River up from the Sandfly Bay estuary and here you can climb down to the river and scramble upstream to a waterfall. After climbing out of the Falls River the track weaves in and out of ridges before descending to Torrent Bay. Follow along the main beach to pick up a marked path through the settlement of baches. Depending on the tide, paths lead either to the lagoon or to the all-tides track at the eastern end of the settlement. Anchorage Hut can be reached 2 hours either side of low tide by heading across the lagoon from the main jetty at the settlement to the south-eastern corner of the lagoon where a track leads over a small ridge to Anchorage Beach. Alternatively the all-tides track can be used to reach this point, though this is a far longer route. Anchorage Hut (DOC, 26 bunks, wood stove) is at the far end of the beach with a large area for camping adjacent to the hut.

Anchorage Hut to Marahau: 3–4 hours, Grade 1.

The Coast Track to Marahau can be joined by a variety of routes. If using the tidal route across Torrent Bay lagoon the track starts in the southeastern corner of the lagoon. The all-tides track around the lagoon leads directly onto the Coast Track. From Anchorage Hut another route starts midway along the beach, climbs up beyond the swamp and meets the Coast Track some distance inland. Winding over ridges and in and out of gullies the Coast Track emerges onto the coast above Astrolabe Roadstead, the stretch of water between Adele and Fisherman Islands and the mainland. Between here and Marahau there are many side-tracks down to the beaches below, with campsites at Appletree Bay and above Tinline Bay. Past Tinline Bay fire has destroyed the forest and the track passes through shrubland to the head of the estuary and the causeway across to Marahau carpark at the end of the Coast Track.

THE INLAND TRACKS

The tracks that wind into the hill country above Abel Tasman's coastline offer a good contrast to the gentle meanderings of the Coast Track. These tracks are more typical of New Zealand tramping, with harder walking and far less use. Trampers paying for use of the huts on the inland tracks require either a Backcountry Pass or DOC hut tickets.

Coast Track to Moa Park Hut (1010 m) via Castle Rocks Shelter (700 m): 6½ hours, Grade 2.

Holyoake Clearing on the route to Castle Rocks Shelter can be reached via two tracks off the Coast Track. The better track leaves from Tinline Bay near the Marahau end. It starts as a benched track but soon becomes a steeper and more strenuous climb. Holyoake Clearing can also be reached from the Torrent Bay area of the Coast Track on a patchy track that leaves from either the all-tides track around Torrent Bay Lagoon, east of the bridge over the Torrent River, or from the Coast Track south of the Anchorage Hut turn-off. Holyoake Clearing is mainly an area of bracken and gorse, and hosts the dilapidated Holyoake Clearing Shelter (which gives only basic shelter) with good views down to the coast. Above the clearing the going becomes more pleasant as the track weaves through a tangled system of forested granite ridges to Castle Rocks Shelter (DOC, 8 bunks, wood stove), 5 hours from the coast. A short scramble out to the Castle Rocks gives spreading views out over Tasman Bay.

Above Castle Rocks Hut the track climbs steadily up to the southern end of Moa Park, a natural clearing of tussock fringed by high-altitude beech forest. On the track to the Moa Park Hut (DOC, 4 bunks, open fire) two side-tracks lead off to granite tors (outcrops) with fine views.

Moa Park Hut (1010 m) to Pigeon Saddle (310 m), Totaranui Road, via Awapoto Hut (606 m): 7 hours, Grade 2.
This track heads down toward the coast along the Evans Ridge, enclosed for much of the way beneath the forest canopy. From the northern end of Moa Park pick up the track which undulates across the hilltop called Sub A and descends to Awapoto Hut (DOC, 12 bunks, wood stove) sitting astride the ridge $4^{1}/_{2}$ hours from Moa Park Hut. Below Awapoto Hut the track emerges from the forest near Centre Peak before reaching the road at Pigeon Saddle. There is a signposted water source 1 hour and 15 minutes above Awapoto Hut, but no water below the hut.

Canaan carpark (730 m) to Moa Park Hut (1010 m): 2 hours, Grade 2.
From the picnic and camping area at the Canaan carpark follow the marked track skirting around farmland to the Wainui Saddle. Past the saddle the track crosses the forested Evans Ridge and drops to the Moa Park Hut (DOC, 4 bunks, open fire).

Canaan carpark (730 m) to Rameka Road (121 m) via Rameka Track: 3–4 hours, Grade 2.
The Rameka Track is an old benched pack track that leaves the Moa Park track a short way from the carpark. It keeps to an easy line, descending through beech forest to emerge at the top of a farm road that leads down for 6 km to the sealed Rameka Road in the Takaka Valley, a further 6 km from Takaka.

Canaan carpark (730 m) to Clifton (30 m) via Wainui Track and Bird's Clearing: $5^{1}/_{2}$ hours, Grade 2.
Initially following the track to Moa Park the Wainui Track splits off this track to drop into the upper reaches of the Wainui River. A pleasant walk leads through some of the finest beech forest in the park to the Wainui Hut (DOC, 4 bunks, open fire), $1^{1}/_{2}$ hours from the Canaan carpark. Below the hut the track climbs out on to the Pikikiruna Range and descends onto farmland and eventually Clifton. Below Wainui Hut another track ascends onto the Evans Ridge to connect with the track between Moa Park and the Awapoto Hut.

kahurangi *national park*

At 452,000 hectares Kahurangi National Park is New Zealand's second largest park and one of the country's most significant havens for native plants and wildlife. Kahurangi is also New Zealand's most recent national park, formed in the mid-1990s from a sequence of forest parks and reserves in the South Island's vast, remote and mountainous northwest, between the Buller River and Farewell Spit.

Mountainous, forested, glaciated, deeply dissected, coastal Kahurangi has unparalleled landscape and geological diversity, with natural values of international standing. Hundreds of millions of years ago Kahurangi was joined to Fiordland until the same forces that raised the Southern Alps skewed Fiordland and Kahurangi 450 km apart along the edges of the Alpine Fault. The mountains of Kahurangi were formed by block faulting along several major faultlines, and the highest peak (Mt Owen in the eastern-lying Marino Mountains) is 1875 m. These are not high mountains by Southern Alps standards, but large and recently formed earthquake slips and lakes are evidence that earth-building forces are still very active in this part of New Zealand, with major earthquakes causing significant landslides in the park as recently as 1929 and 1968. Geologists have discovered in the park New Zealand's oldest fossils, its oldest (500 million years) and most diverse assemblage of rock types, and the oldest evidence of volcanic activity. They have identified the broad expanses of the Mt Arthur Tablelands and the Gouland Downs as the country's oldest landforms, formed under the sea and lifted to their present heights. The park's karst (waterworn marble and limestone) landscapes are the most extensive in the country, and cave systems beneath Mt Owen and the Arthur Range include the Southern Hemisphere's deepest and longest. Mt Owen is ranked one of the finest examples of glaciated karst in the Southern Hemisphere. Ice age glaciers shaped the topography in many areas of the park, but other sectors escaped the ice, allowing plants and wildlife to flourish where they were wiped out in other parts of the South Island.

The presence of widely ranging rock types and topography has enabled the

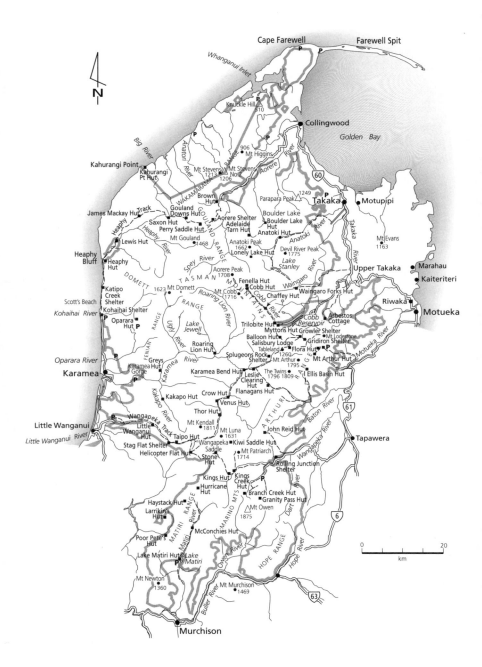

evolution of an exceptional range of plants and wildlife. Despite the recent destructive impact of human-introduced pests, Kahurangi remains a sanctuary for 1220, or 50 per cent, of all recorded plant species in New Zealand, many either nationally rare or endemic; and 80 per cent of New Zealand's alpine plant species, 48 per cent of which are endemic. Forest covers 85 per cent of the park, a mosaic of upland beech forests and lowland and coastal forests of mixed podocarp, beech and hardwood species. Sequences of intact ecosystems from coastal margins through forests to alpine zones are rare anywhere in New Zealand. Forests, wetlands and alpine zones sustain over 100 native bird species, including many threatened with extinction such as the great spotted kiwi, blue duck, rock wren, fernbird and yellow-crowned parakeet; among invertebrates are 'living fossils' like the giant land snail, and the largest of New Zealand's spiders, the Nelson cave spider, an inhabitant of limestone caves underneath Oparara's lowland forests.

Maori settlement, dating back 700–800 years, was predominantly along coastal areas of the park, usually at rivermouths and estuaries where food supplies were good. The site of a coastal village at the Heaphy rivermouth of importance to Ngai Tahu is excluded from the park. Use by Maori of the hinterland is thought to have been limited to seasonal food gathering, or to travel routes linking the West Coast with Nelson. A number of battles between tribes were fought on the margins of the park in the early 1800s. Abel Tasman and Captain James Cook sailed past and described the northwest during their exploratory voyages in the seventeenth and eighteenth centuries, but it was gangs of Australian sealers who were the first Europeans into the area around 1803, clubbing an existence around the coast until the 1840s. Looking inland Europeans eyed the park's potential mineral resources from an early stage, and gold discovered in 1860 in the Aorere Valley initiated New Zealand's first gold rush. Most of the present complex of tracks through the interior, such as the Heaphy and Wangapeka, date to efforts in the 1800s to support miners and graziers. Such routes were benched wide and followed easy contours, a legacy enjoyed by today's trampers. Miners' interest in the northwest continued until the late 1980s but no significant finds were made. Keeping miners from the area was an important factor motivating conservationists promoting national park protection; hydro-development and roadbuilding proposals were other factors in the debate. Logging took place right around the park's margins until as late as 1986.

Kahurangi's ranges offer superb tramping opportunities, from day walks and relatively easy tramps to multi-day struggles through untracked wilderness. Trampers can choose between long, forested valley journeys or ridge and mountain traverses amid expanding vistas across the park. Over 500 km of walking tracks and routes are available, serviced by almost 50 huts. The most popular walks are the Heaphy Track, Wangapeka Track, the route to the Mt Arthur Tablelands, and in the Cobb Valley. Other routes offer good access onto the tops — Mt Owen, Mt Arthur and the Matiri plateaux in particular. In the north the Tasman Mountains are the focal point of the Tasman Wilderness Area which was founded in 1987, 80,000 ha of untracked and challenging country for the experienced tramper.

Depending on your choice of route tramping is possible year-round in Kahurangi. Long periods of stable weather are not uncommon during summer or winter months, but trampers should be prepared for heavy rain and snow. Frontal rain sweeps the park from the south, pouring between 4000 mm and 5600 mm onto mountain areas every year. On the major routes rivers and sidestreams are bridged, but away from these care must be taken when crossing rivers. Snow falls at any time of the year but only in winter are the tops snowbound for long periods. Temperatures vary — inland valleys which are warm and humid through summer suffer severe frosts in winter. West coast temperatures tend to be mild all year. The prevailing wind is from the northwest, and western-northwestern coastal parts receive a strong and constant battering. Kahurangi is less well known as a tramping destination but those who make the effort will discover a range and quality of wilderness experiences matched only by those in Fiordland.

Information

PARK INFORMATION CENTRES AND AREA OFFICES

Kahurangi National Park is serviced by both the Nelson and West Coast conservancies of the Department of Conservation. There is no central visitor centre, but rather a series of area offices and information centres around the park in Nelson, Motueka, Takaka, Murchison, Westport and Karamea from where information can be sought.

General information about all areas of the park can be sought from:

Nelson Visitor Information Centre
Corner Trafalgar and Halifax Streets
Box 788
Nelson
Phone (03) 546 9335
Fax (03) 548 2805

For information on the Mt Arthur Tablelands, Baton and Wangapeka Valleys, and northern approaches to Mt Owen, contact:

Motueka Area Office
Corner King Edward and High Streets
PO Box 97
Motueka
Phone (03) 528 9117
Fax (03) 528 6751

Their hours are: 1 March–31 October: 8.00 a.m.–12.00 noon, 1.00 p.m.–4.30 p.m. Monday to Friday; 1 November–28 February: 8.00 a.m.–5.00 p.m. Monday to Friday. For information on the Golden Bay sector of the park including the Cobb, Waingaro, Anatoki and Aorere (northern access to the Heaphy Track and Boulder Lake) valleys, and Kahurangi Point contact:

Golden Bay Area Office
62 Commercial Street
PO Box 166
Takaka
Phone (03) 525 8026
Fax (03) 525 8444

Their hours are: Peak summer months: 8.00 a.m.–4.00 p.m. seven days a week; off season: 8.00 a.m.–4.00 p.m. Monday–Friday. For information on southern approaches to Mt Owen and the Matiri Valley contact:

Murchison Field Base
Fairfax Street
RD 3
Murchison
Phone/fax (03) 523 9106

Hours 8.00 a.m.–4.30 p.m. Monday to Friday. For information on southern approaches to the Heaphy Track, Oparara Valley area, and the Wangapeka contact:

Karamea Visitor Information Centre
Box 94
Karamea
Phone/fax (03) 782 6652

ACCESS

There are numerous roads providing good two-wheel-drive access to the park's northern, eastern, southern and southwestern areas. Many of these roads, however, are unsealed and are subject to slips, snow conditions and in some cases flooding.

Northern areas of the park are reached from Golden Bay off SH 60 from Nelson. The Cobb and Upper Takaka valleys are reached by a signposted road at Upper Takaka. One kilometre south of Collingwood, the Aorere Valley road is the access route to the Heaphy Track, Boulder Lake road end, Kaituna Track and to the Aorere Goldfields (all of which are well signposted).

The Mt Arthur Tablelands, the Wangapeka Track and northern approaches to Mt Owen are all reached from SH 61 in the Motueka Valley between Motueka and Kohatu. Turn off at Tapawera to reach the Wangapeka Track and Mt Owen. To reach Graham Saddle for access to Mt Arthur, turn off at Woodstock or Ngatimoti to reach the west bank of the Motueka River and follow signs to the Graham Valley.

The southern approaches to Mt Owen are via the Owen Valley off SH 6 just below the Owen River Hotel. To reach the Matiri Valley turn west off SH 6 at the Mangles Bridge 5 km north of Murchison.

The approach to the southern end of the Heaphy Track and the Oparara Valley is from Karamea, on the coast north of Westport.

TRANSPORT SERVICES

Being major tourist destinations Nelson, Golden Bay and the West Coast are all well served by bus services between the principal centres. Major airlines operate daily flights to Nelson and Westport, while smaller operators also fly to Motueka, Takaka and Karamea, including Nelson Aero Club (phone (03) 547 9643), Tasman Bay Aviation (phone (03) 547 2378), and Abel Tasman Aviation (phone 0800 304 560). Minibus transport for trampers is provided in Nelson and Golden Bay by Kahurangi Trampers Service (phone (03) 528 9461 or (03) 544 1169), while the Last Resort (phone toll free 0800 505 042) can arrange a variety of transport around Karamea. Abel Tasman Coachlines (phone (03) 548 0285) run a bus service to Takaka. Collingwood Safari Tours (phone (03) 524 8257) run a service from Collingwood up to the beginning of the Heaphy Track, as does Kahurangi Bus Services (phone (03) 525 9434).

ACCOMMODATION

Camping areas: Within the park there are free camping sites (in some cases outside road end huts) with minimal facilities at either end of the Wangapeka Track, Rolling River (northern approach to Mt Owen), Cobb Valley road end, Matiri and Owen Valleys (both with permission from landowner). On the Heaphy Track camping is permitted at three sites on the coastal section only. Passes are required for these. Free roadside camping areas can be found on SH 6 at Mangles Bridge just north of Murchison, at Norris Gully about 3 km towards Nelson from Kohatu; several sites along SH 61 in the Motueka Valley;

at Ruby Bay 3 km north of Mapua on SH 60. There is free camping in the Cobb Valley at two sites.

Campgrounds: Serviced campgrounds can be found in Nelson, Motueka, Tapawera, Pohara (near Takaka), Collingwood, Pakawau, Murchison, Westport, Karamea. Free camping is possible at most park road ends.

Hotels/motels: All major towns have a range of accommodation from luxury to backpacker and bed and breakfast.

SERVICES

There are no services within the park. Petrol and supplies are available from all major towns around the park.

WEATHER

Like any westerly-lying region in New Zealand, Kahurangi receives its fair share of wet weather as moist air flows cross the South Island from the west and south. Mountainous areas receive 4000–5600 mm of rain a year but the plains east of the park receive half this amount. Trampers should be prepared for periods of heavy rain. Some of the best periods of settled weather can be expected in mid to late summer. Snow falls in the park during winter and in high snow years some tracks are impassable. Prevailing winds in summer are from the northwest and, during winter, east to southeast or southwest. Variable wind conditions are not uncommon given the park's high mountains and deep valleys which cause considerable wind turbulence. Winds can be particularly strong in western and northwestern coastal areas.

MAPS

Parkmap 273 of Kahurangi National Park covers the entire park and has huts and tracks marked. For more detailed information trampers should use the Topomap 260 series M25 Collingwood, M26 Cobb, M26 Heaphy, M27 Mt Arthur, L27 Karamea, M28 Wangapeka, L28 Mokihinui, and M29 Murchison.

FURTHER READING

The North West Nelson Tramping Guide by Derek Shaw (Nikau Press, 1991) is a comprehensive tramping guide to the area which also offers an excellent narrative on the park's natural and human history. Derek Shaw's *Golden Bay Walks* and *Buller Walks* by Terry Sumner, both also published by Nikau Press, are good guides to short walks in the park and other areas. The Department of Conservation has also published pamphlets and brochures on specific areas of the park.

Short walks

WALKS IN GOLDEN BAY
Parapara Peak Track: 6–8 hours return, Grade 3–4.
You need to allow a full day for this stiff climb to Parapara Peak (1240 m), but you will be rewarded with splendid views of Golden Bay. Access is via Ward-Holmes Road just northwest of Puramahoi on SH 60 between Takaka and Collingwood. From the carpark, the track crosses the river and zigzags into Copperstain Creek. Look for the benched track on the right that emerges 10 minutes up the creekbed. Take special care to note the route on this next section as several old logging roads intersect with the track. At a slip 20 minutes from the creek, the track climbs onto a ridge, which is then followed to the peak. It is advisable to carry water on this climb.

WALKS IN THE AORERE VALLEY
Kaituna Walk: 1–2 hours return, Grade 1.
Drive 5 km beyond Rockville and turn onto Carter's Road, following signs to the track start where there is a delightful family walk through magnificent rainforest to the Kaituna River forks. Huge rata and kahikatea trees, and historic mining relics, are a feature of this walk.
Kaituna Track: 8 hours, Grade 3–4.
This track offers an excellent crossing of the Wakamarama Range between the Aorere Valley and Whanganui Inlet, with commanding views from the tops, interesting forest and pakihi flora and wildlife. It can be walked in either direction. Start as for the Kaituna Walk (above) or from Knuckle Hill which is signposted off the road around the eastern side of Whanganui Inlet.
Mt Stevens (1213 m), 6–7 hours return, Grade 3–4.
This is a steep route from the Aorere Valley to Mt Stevens on the Wakamarama Range with good views from the top. The route begins about 1 km south of 15 Mile Creek on the Bainham-Heaphy Track road. Water should be carried on this climb.

WALKS FROM THE BROWN RIVER CARPARK, NORTHERN END OF THE HEAPHY TRACK
Close to the Brown River carpark at the Bainham end of the Heaphy Track is an interesting short walk and a good day walk.
Brown River Nature Walk: 15 minutes, Grade 1.
South of the carpark, this easy stroll meanders through tall forest including kahikatea, matai and red beech.

Shakespeare Flat: 6–7 hours return, Grade 2.
The trip to Shakespeare Flat is an enjoyable day walk to the Upper Aorere Valley, notable for its splendid forest and abundant birdlife. Follow the Heaphy Track from Brown Hut for 1¹/₂ hours to the Shakespeare Flat turn-off then descend for an hour to Shakespeare Flat.

WALKS AROUND THE COBB VALLEY

The tracks in the Cobb Valley begin from the access road to the Cobb Reservoir from Upper Takaka. To reach the area from Nelson turn south off SH 60 at Upper Takaka and follow the road past the Cobb Power Station and up to the Cobb Reservoir. Trilobite Hut is at the road end at the western end of the reservoir. This steep winding metal road is occasionally closed because of slips or snow conditions. Check with DOC for road conditions before travelling.

Asbestos Forest Walk: 1 hour, Grade 1.
This is an easy beech forest walk that begins 2 km from the Cobb power station. The walk ends at a waterfall and returns by the same route.

Asbestos Cottage via Asbestos Track: 2–3 hours, Grade 2.
Begin as for the Asbestos Forest Walk (above) but continue past the waterfall to an abandoned mine, and then on to historic Asbestos Cottage. A slip just beyond the waterfall requires care. From the cottage, a track climbs to the Cobb Ridge Track (see below), and another continues for 20 minutes to the Bullock Track (see below).

Cobb Ridge Track to Lake Peel: 6–7 hours return, Grade 2–3.
This track provides a magnificent day walk encompassing beech and cedar forests, and alpine tussock grasslands, with good views of the Cobb Valley area, the Mt Arthur range and the Upper Takaka Valley. The track leaves the Cobb Road from the highpoint overlooking the Cobb Dam and reservoir. After 2 hours it intersects with the Bullock Track which is followed briefly north to Peat Flat. (The Bullock Track also allows a fast descent to the reservoir and a return along the road to the start point.) From Peat Flat the track eventually emerges onto tussocklands, and follows along a poled route to reach Lake Peel after 2–3 hours. Return via the same route.

Cobb Valley to Upper Takaka Valley via the Bullock Track: 2–3 hours, Grade 2–3.
The Bullock Track is an old drovers' route. It begins off the road alongside the reservoir and climbs steeply at first to Peat Flat, over the Cobb Ridge and descends to Broken Ridge. From here a return trip can be made to the reservoir via Asbestos Cottage or by continuing along the Asbestos Track and Cobb Road back to the reservoir.

Sylvester and Diamond Lakes: 6–7 hours return, Grade 1.

From the western side of the Cobb Reservoir allow 2–3 hours up a disused four-wheel-drive track to reach Bushline Hut (DOC, 5 bunks, wood stove) at the edge of Sylvester Basin. From here exploratory trips can be made to the nearby Sylvester Lakes or further to the Diamond Lakes set among tussock grasslands beneath Iron Mountain.

WALKS AROUND MOUNT ARTHUR

Because the Flora carpark underneath Mt Arthur is at a height of 930 m it offers relatively easy access for day trips into nearby beautiful alpine areas.

Mt Arthur Hut (1300 m) 3–4 hours return, Grade 1–2.

This is a popular and not too strenuous day trip through beech and dracophyllum forests to the alpine zone below Mt Arthur. From Flora carpark walk 10 minutes to Flora Saddle. Here the Mt Arthur Track branches left, climbing steadily up a well-graded benched path to the Mt Arthur Hut (DOC, 6 bunks, gas cooking and heating) which is reached after 1–1¹/₂ hours. The alpine zone immediately above the hut is well worth exploring for its varied alpine plantlife, karst formations and fine views.

Mt Arthur (1795 m): 5–6 hours return, Grade 3.

This is a highly recommended and, in good weather, relatively straightforward alpine tramp to one of the park's highest points, with spectacular views of the park, Tasman Bay and the Richmond Range behind Nelson. For those interested in alpine flora this is an ideal area to visit with alpine flowers at their best from late spring through summer. Follow the route described above to Mt Arthur Hut. From here continue along the well-worn poled route, initially along the broad tussocked Arthur Ridge leading south to Mt Arthur. Higher up the path enters the area of exposed glaciated marble outcrops below Mt Arthur, winding past sinkholes and slots. The track sidles beneath the northern slopes of Winter Peak around the head of Horseshoe Basin before reaching the short steep scramble onto Mt Arthur's summit plateau. The walk from Mt Arthur Hut to the summit takes about 2 hours, but allow longer if interested in exploring the area a little further. Walkers should be prepared for bad weather, and should not attempt this route in winter without climbing experience and appropriate equipment.

Flora Hut: 2 hours return, Grade 1.

Popular with families, this pleasant walk follows the Flora Track, a road constructed by the Forest Service. It winds through beech forest to reach Flora Hut (12 bunks, open fire) after 30–40 minutes' easy walking from Flora carpark. This is a good place for a picnic and a dip in the Flora Stream. In winter the slope behind the hut is a popular tobogganing run.

Mt Arthur Hut via Flora Hut: 2 hours, Grade 1–3.

Follow as above to Flora Hut. Behind Flora Hut a track climbs directly to Mt Arthur Hut. Walkers can complete a circuit back to Flora carpark by returning down the Mt Arthur Track (see p. 42).

Mt Lodestone and Flora Hut: 4 hour round trip, Grade 2–3.

From Flora carpark, the track north to Mt Lodestone is initially steep, lays back in its middle section then steepens again before reaching the top, which at 1462 m is crowned by tussocks. From the summit there are panoramic views to be enjoyed before descending down the southwestern ridge to Flora Hut and returning along the Flora Track to the carpark.

Gordon's Pyramid via Clouston's Track: 7–8 hours return, Grade 3.

This more strenuous trip to Gordon's Pyramid continues past Flora Hut (see above) reaching the junction of Clouston's Track 40 minutes from the hut. Clouston's Track is a well-graded track constructed in 1911 to service Clouston's Mine. The mine entrance, tailings and other relics are found on the bush edge. From the mine a poled route leads to Gordon's Pyramid, which is reached about 4 hours from the carpark. Another poled route from the mine follows the bush edge and then descends towards Salisbury Lodge on the Mt Arthur Tablelands 1–1½ hours (see p. 53). For those comfortable traversing open alpine country, an interesting circuit back to Flora carpark can be completed from Gordon's Pyramid by following the poled route tending southeast along Pyramid Ridge to below Mt Arthur. The route crosses Horseshoe Basin and gains Arthur Ridge about 30 minutes above Mt Arthur Hut.

WALKS FROM COURTHOUSE FLAT IN THE WANGAPEKA VALLEY

Courthouse Flat is 10 minutes' drive up the Rolling River from Rolling River Junction. Several day walks are possible here and camping is allowed at the flat.

Blue Creek resurgence: 1 hour return, Grade 1.

This is a pleasant interpreted walk from Courthouse Flat past open grassy flats and through forest to where the waters of Blue Creek emerge, having flowed underground for several kilometres from near Granity Pass. Numerous old mining relics, including a quartz-crushing battery and other machinery, and tailings and races dating back to the 1860s, are passed along the way.

Nuggety Creek: 2 hours return, Grade 1–2.

From the carpark this longer walk takes in old miners' hut sites and mining relics. The track is initially wide and easily followed but some narrow sections must also be traversed.

WALKS IN THE MATIRI VALLEY

Lake Matiri: 4–5 hours return, Grade 2.

This is a relatively easy walk from the Matiri Valley carpark. Follow the marked route along the true right bank of the Matiri to a ford over the west branch of the Matiri River, usually straightforward in normal weather. The track is wide and easily followed, and shortly before Lake Matiri it climbs over a high point before descending to the hut (KNP, 6 bunks, open fire) above the lake-edge. This is a lovely spot for lunch and a good base for exploratory walks in the lake environs, notable for a variety of native and introduced waterfowl.

WALKS FROM KOHAIHAI

Fifteen kilometres north of Karamea, Kohaihai is at the southern end of the Heaphy Track. There are several short walks from the Kohaihai Shelter.

Nikau Walk: 40 minutes, Grade 1.

This walk gives a choice of loop walks through fine West Coast forest next to the Kohaihai River. The walks begin on the Heaphy Track, but branches off just over the Kohaihai swingbridge.

Lookout Walk: 30 minutes return, Grade 1.

This short walk begins at the Kohaihai Shelter, climbing in a zigzag to a point overlooking the Kohaihai rivermouth. There is a picnic table at the top, and good views out over the Tasman Sea.

Scott's Beach: 2 hours return, Grade 1–2.

This popular short walk takes walkers to the first of the sweeping beaches that fringe the forests at the southern end of the Heaphy Track. From Kohaihai Shelter follow the Heaphy Track to the Kohaihai Saddle before descending to the beach. An alternative route to the beach is possible from the saddle down Fisherman's Track, where seals are sometimes seen on the rocks at the entrance to the beach.

Katipo Creek Shelter: 6 hours return, Grade 2.

For those wanting to follow the Heaphy Track further north than Scott's Beach (see above), Katipo Creek Shelter is a good day-trip objective, and gives a fine experience of this beautiful and unspoilt forested coastline.

WALKS IN THE UPPER OPARARA VALLEY

Two dramatic and beautiful limestone arches are the highlights of the walks in this wonderful forested valley, which was threatened by logging in the relatively recent past. To reach them drive 8 km north of Karamea and turn right just before Break Creek, following a road signposted to the arches and the Honeycomb Hill Caves. Skirt a sawmill and continue for 16 km along a metal road (passable by most vehicles) over a steep saddle and down to the

Oparara River and a carpark where tracks lead to two of the three arches.

Oparara Arch: 40 minutes return, Grade 1.

An easy gravelled path leaving opposite the carpark leads upstream along the Oparara River through mixed beech and podocarp forest to the largest of the arches in this area. The first sight of this 43-metre-high arch is awe-inspiring. The Oparara River flows 200 m through the arch, which is 49 m at its widest point. It's possible to scramble through the arch to the other side.

Little Arch: 1¹/₂ hours return, Grade 2.

Also known as Elven Door, this arch is reached along the track that goes downstream from the carpark. Not as well defined as the previous route, it climbs a limestone ridge and eventually crosses the top of the arch before descending to the river.

Mirror Tarn: 40 minutes return, Grade 1.

North of the carpark, a track leads to this sheltered forest lake.

Box Canyon and Crazy Paving Caves: 20 minutes return, Grade 1.

A further 3 km drive from the Arch carpark a sign indicates the start of this walk to a small limestone cave system. Take a torch, and stay on the formed path through the cave.

WALKS IN THE LOWER OPARARA VALLEY

The lower Oparara is the site of three interesting walks through forests, limestone scenery and historic goldmining relics in the Fenian Basin. The tracks all begin from the same point, reached from Karamea by following signs to Oparara for 5 km from Market Cross. Alternatively, from the road to the Heaphy Track, take the side-road that follows the south bank of the Oparara River.

Fenian Creek: 2 hours return, Grade 2.

From the limestone quarry follow the broad benched track up the Oparara Gorge. Maloney's Bluff, an impressive viewpoint above the river, is reached in about 45 minutes. From here the track descends to cross Cavern Creek. Fenian Creek is 50 m on from Cavern Creek.

Adams Flat: 4 hours return, Grade 2.

Follow the route described above to Fenian Creek. Adams Flat is a further hour's walk beyond Fenian Creek through tall podocarp and beech forest. The track climbs gently to a terrace and the site of a Depression-era settlement.

Cavern Creek Loop: 3 hours return, Grade 2.

Follow the route to Fenian Creek described above. Just beyond Cavern Creek, turn right onto a well marked loop track which passes broken limestone outcrops and through or past several caves including the 170-metre-long Tunnel Cave. Take a torch and warm clothing for the caves.

Tramping trip summary

The following summary outlines most of the recognised tramping trips undertaken in Kahurangi National Park. Used with the route descriptions that follow, it can provide a basis for planning a tramp. Remember, however, that these are only suggestions and by using a map and consulting DOC staff many variations on these tramps can be found. The times given make no allowances for delays caused by bad weather.

- Beginning at Anatori River on West Coast south of Whanganui Inlet to Kahurangi Point Lighthouse and keeper's residence via coastal beach route. Return the same way (2 days).
- Heaphy Track, beginning at Aorere Valley road end through to Karamea on the West Coast (4–5 days).
- Beginning at Aorere Valley from James Road, Brown Cow Ridge to Boulder Lake and return by same route (2 days).
- Beginning at Aorere Valley from James Road to Anatoki Valley via Brown Cow Ridge, Boulder Lake, Adelaide Tarn and Yuletide Ridge (4 days).
- Beginning at the Anatoki Valley, through trip to Takaka Valley via Anatoki and Waingaro Tracks (3–4 days).
- Beginning from Cobb Reservoir, to Bushline Hut and Sylvester Lakes. Return by same route (2 days).
- Beginning from Cobb Reservoir, from Trilobite Hut up Cobb Valley to Cobb and Fenella Huts, returning by same route (2 days).
- Beginning from Cobb Reservoir, through trip to Flora carpark from Cobb Road, Myttons Hut, via Lake Peel, Balloon Hut, Salisbury Lodge, down Balloon Creek and up Flora Stream to Flora carpark (2 days). Alternatively, return to Cobb Reservoir from Salisbury Lodge via Upper and Lower Junctions on Takaka River and up Bullock Track (2 days). If returning to reservoir via track from Asbestos Cottage, allow extra 2–4 hours.
- Mt Arthur Tablelands, beginning from Flora Saddle, Flora Track to Salisbury Lodge and return via Gordon's Pyramid, and Mt Arthur Track (2 days).
- Mt Arthur Tablelands through to Wangapeka Track, beginning from Flora Saddle, through to Wangapeka Valley via Flora and Leslie Tracks to Karamea Bend, up Karamea Valley to Wangapeka Track, and exit to Tapawera or West Coast along the Wangapeka Track (5–6 days).
- Beginning from Baton Valley, up Baton Valley to Flanagans Hut and Baton Saddle and return by same route (2 days).

- Wangapeka Track, beginning from Wangapeka Valley road end, up Wangapeka Valley over Wangapeka Saddle, around headwaters of the Karamea Valley, up the Taipo Valley and cross into the Little Whanganui valley via Little Whanganui Saddle to the West Coast (3–4 days).
- Beginning from Wangapeka Valley, up Wangapeka Track to Kiwi Stream, then up to Kiwi Saddle, cross to Mt Luna and return to Wangapeka Valley via Stone Track (3 days). Alternatively, return to Rolling River via Kiwi Stream or via Mt Patriarch, and Gibbs or Chummies tracks (2 days).
- Mt Owen, beginning from Courthouse Flat, to Granity Pass via Billies Knob Track, climb Mt Owen and return by same route or via Cullifords Hill (2 days).
- 1000 Acre Plateau, beginning from Lake Matiri, climb onto 100 and 1000 Acre Plateaux, climb Needle and Haystack and return same way (3–4 days).
- Beginning from Lake Matiri, up Matiri Valley to Lake Jeanette and Hurricane Hut. Return same way (3 days).

Tramping

Golden Bay
KAHURANGI POINT LIGHTHOUSE

This is a unique coastal walk along huge West Coast beaches to the Kahurangi Point lighthouse, and the old keeper's residence (the house is now run by the Department of Conservation). This walk is normally done as an overnight walk from the Anatori River, and as it involves three river crossings, is best done when the tide is ebbing. The walk must be timed so that Big River is crossed at dead low tide, otherwise the crossing is too deep. (Tide times here are roughly the same as those for Nelson.) To reach the Anatori River from Golden Bay, turn left at Seaford just north of Pakawau and drive the very scenic route around Whanganui Inlet. The road eventually reaches Patarau on the West Coast. Continue driving southwest to the Anatori River approximately 12 km from Patarau. Those with four-wheel-drive vehicles can cross the Anatori and continue a further 5 km to Te Rata Creek, or 8 km to the Turamawiwi River, both of which provide access to the coast. There are camping sites on the banks of the Anatori River.

Anatori River to Kahurangi Point: 4–5 hours, Grade 2.

Cross the Anatori River (straightforward in normal flows) and head to the beach. Continue southwards along the beach, crossing the Turamawiwi and Anaweka Rivers at the safest-looking fords near their mouths. There is no way around the Anaweka's wide estuary. At Big River move inland around the estuary and cross at its widest point at dead low tide. There may be a crossing point marked by drivers of four-wheel-drive vehicles. At Kahurangi Point the old keeper's house (KNP, 17 bunks, coal range) backs onto coastal dunes and forest. Good camping sites are found in front of the house.

THE HEAPHY TRACK

The Heaphy Track traverses the northwest corner of Kahurangi National Park, joining Golden Bay with North Westland's Nikau Coast. Officially a Great Walk, the Heaphy is well graded and benched, passes through mixed podocarp/beech forests, alpine tussocklands and some of New Zealand's oldest geological formations. It thoroughly deserves its reputation as one of the country's finest tramping routes. More recently the track has been the subject of some controversy over its use by mountain-bikers, an activity banned when the area became a national park. The area is also under (a fairly remote) threat from tourism interests and developers who are proposing to construct a road through the region traversed by the Heaphy, linking Karamea with Collingwood.

The Heaphy Track is described below from north to south. It can be walked from either end, but most favour leaving the coastal section of the track till last, as it is one of its major highlights. It is 82 km long and trampers usually take 4–6 days to complete it. The Heaphy is primarily a summer route and may well be blocked by snow during winter. Camping is permitted on the coastal section only. A Heaphy track hut pass must be purchased to stay in the seven huts or a camp pass to stay at a campsite. Given the high usage of this track, carrying a tent is advisable, especially during peak summer months.

Brown Hut (122 m) to Perry Saddle (868 m): 5–6 hours, Grade 1.
From Brown Hut (DOC, 20 bunks, open fire) follow the track across a paddock to the start of the climb to Perry Saddle, 17 km away. The track is well graded and soon enters the forest. The turn-off to Shakespeare Flat is passed after 1¹/₂ hours, and Aorere Shelter is reached in 4 hours (KNP, 3 platforms). There are fine views of the park, Golden Bay and the North Island from here. Three kilometres on, a lookout at Flanagans Corner (915 m, the track's highest point) allows views over the Upper Aorere Valley, Mt Olympus and the Anatoki Range. Perry Saddle Hut (DOC, 26 bunks, gas stoves) is another 30 minutes on.

Perry Saddle to Gouland Downs Hut (610 m): 2–3 hours, Grade 1.
After a short rise, the track descends all the way to Gouland Downs. The downs are an ancient limestone peneplain, lifted from the seafloor and topped by scattered granite outcrops, spiky scrub, tussocks and subalpine bog plants. The limestone surface is scored by numerous deeply cut streamways and has many deep potholes to be wary of, if venturing off the track. Gouland Downs Hut

(DOC, 10 bunks, open fire) was built in 1936. Several nearby limestone arches and the resurgence of a small stream from a cave are worth exploring.

Gouland Downs Hut to Saxon Hut (670 m): 1$^1/_2$–2 hours, Grade 1.

From the hut the track takes a gentle line across the downs, through patches of beech forest, scrub and flax to Saxon Hut (DOC, 16 bunks, gas cookers) on the western edge of the downs at the head of the Saxon Valley.

Saxon Hut to Mackay Hut (695 m): 3–3$^1/_2$ hours, Grade 1.

Beyond Saxon Hut the track descends to flats on the Saxon River, then climbs to a broad ridge between Gouland and Mackay Downs, the latter named for the explorer who campaigned for the construction of the route that is now the Heaphy. (A wet weather alternative to the first section of track, prone to flooding, is marked 400 m from Saxon Hut.) Turning southwest on the edge of Mackay Downs, the track undulates through tussock and beech forest to reach Mackay Hut (DOC, 26 bunks, gas cookers) which overlooks the distant Heaphy River mouth and the Tasman Sea.

Mackay Hut to Lewis Hut (15 m): 3–4 hours, Grade 1.

Leaving the downs' more open landscape the track re-enters forest below the hut and steadily descends into the Heaphy Valley, through increasingly lush West Coast rainforest dominated by rimu and other tall podocarps. Lewis Hut (DOC, 20 bunks, gas cookers) is on the valley floor.

Lewis Hut to Heaphy Hut (5 m): 2$^1/_2$ hours, Grade 1.

Almost 400 m downstream from the hut the track crosses the Heaphy River then follows down the true left of the river to reach Heaphy Hut (DOC, 20 bunks) just back from the coast near the Heaphy River mouth, the site of a former Maori seasonal camp which has been excluded from the park.

Heaphy Hut to Kohaihai Shelter (sea level): 4$^1/_2$–5 hours, Grade 1.

Undoubtedly one of the most enjoyable sections of the walk, the track now follows the coast through corridors of flax and nikau palms, and when tides permit, along long stretches of beach, all the way to the track end at Kohaihai. Two emergency shelters can be used for accommodation if Heaphy Hut is full: Heaphy Shelter, 15 minutes from the hut; and Katipo Creek Shelter, with toilet and fireplace, about halfway to Kohaihai Shelter.

Aorere Valley

Aorere Valley (60 m) to Boulder Lake (1000 m) via the Brown Cow Track: 7–8 hours, Grade 2.

Access is from James Road in the Aorere Valley. Permission is required to cross farmland at the start of the track. Carry sufficient water as there is little to be obtained along the way. From the milking shed at the end of James Road follow a signposted four-wheel-drive track for 2 km (in fact passable by two-wheel-drive vehicles when in good condition) to a carpark and DOC intentions book kiosk. Continue along the now rougher road for another 3 km to a signpost which marks the point where the route enters scrub and forest. About 1¹/₂ km from the signpost, the track turns southwest and soon enters an area of limestone known as 'The Castles'. The track continues to Beathams Clearing (campsites and water of dubious quality) and then climbs up Brown Cow Ridge, sidling around the northern side of Point 926, and moving to the eastern side of the ridge before emerging on Cow Saddle. Following cairns and marker poles leading from the saddle, the route climbs towards then sidles beneath Brown Cow, before descending to Boulder Lake down the ridge between Kiwi and Beak creeks. Boulder Lake Hut (DOC, 8 bunks, wood stove) is at the southern end of the lake next to Suspicion Creek.

Boulder Lake (1000 m) to Adelaide Tarn Hut (1350 m): 5–7 hours, Grade 4.

This is a difficult route that should only be attempted by experienced parties in good weather. From the hut make your way through the tall tussocks lining Arena Creek. Near the head of the creek find the cairns that lead up the wide slope between Arena and Orator Creeks. Below the ridge the route turns south towards Green Saddle. From the saddle, continue south, rounding Point 1450 on the Anatoki (eastern) side of the ridge. At Point 1411, the route sidles again on the eastern side, through forest and open slopes to below the Needles Eye. Climb up to the Needles Eye, and descend steeply to Adelaide Tarn and the tiny hut (DOC, 4 bunks), nestled in a cirque below the dramatic peaks of the Douglas Range. Camping sites can be found above the tarn's outlet. Unmarked routes exist between Adelaide Tarn and Lonely Lake, though these are serious undertakings and should only be attempted by experienced trampers. Contact DOC for route descriptions. See Anatoki Valley section for a description of the route between Anatoki Forks and Adelaide Tarn.

Anatoki Valley

Kotinga Road end (140 m) to Anatoki Forks Hut via the Anatoki Track (625 m): 6–8 hours, Grade 2.

The start of the track is signposted near the end of Kotinga Road, which turns off SH 60 just before Takaka. From the carpark follow markers across farmland and zigzag up a scrubby hillside to a saddle overlooking the Anatoki Valley. From here the well-formed and graded track continues through areas of regenerating and mature forest. The track generally stays well above the river, except when it descends towards Anatoki Bend. The Anatoki Forks Hut (DOC, 6 bunks, woodstove) is situated in a grassy clearing with plenty of campsites.

Anatoki Forks Hut (625 m) to Adelaide Tarn Hut (1350 m): 5–6 hours, Grade 4.

This is a difficult route which should only be undertaken in good weather. This route receives irregular maintenance and is overgrown. Upstream from Anatoki Forks, ford the river and pick up the track that climbs the steep spur separating the two branches of the river. Keeping to the spur, the track emerges onto the tops after an hour, offering fine views. Continue along the ridge, sidling below rocky ribs on the northern side of Yuletide Peak. Cross to the slopes below the Needle, following cairns towards the Needles Eye. When opposite the Eye climb the rocky gut, over the ridge and descend to Adelaide Tarn Hut (DOC, 4 bunks). There are good campsites above the outlet to the tarn.

Anatoki Forks Hut (625 m) to Waingaro/Stanley Forks Hut (725 m): 7–9 hours, Grade 2.

The pack track south of Anatoki Forks follows the true right of the Anatoki River for about an hour. Leaving the main river, the track then begins a steady climb up a major sidestream to a saddle. After 30 to 40 minutes' descent from the saddle, the track reaches a good camping site next to the Stanley River. Between here and Lake Stanley there are a number of swimming holes to be exploited on a hot day. Cross the river and descend the true right to Lake Stanley. Smokey Drip Hut has been removed and it is not safe to camp here. It is a further 3–3¹/₂ hours through forest and gravel flats then a climb to avoid the gorge before the junction of the Waingaro and Stanley rivers to reach the Waingaro/Stanley Forks Hut (DOC, 4 bunks).

Waingaro Valley

Uruwhenua Road to Waingaro Forks Hut (450 m) via the Lockett Range (Waingaro Track): 6–7 hours, Grade 2.

This route into the upper Waingaro Valley begins near the end of Uruwhenua Road in the Takaka Valley. To reach the start of the track, turn off at Lindsay's Bridge, 6 km north of Upper Takaka on SH 60. The track start is signposted 3 km from the bridge. Soon after the initial section of farmland the well-formed track zigzags up the steep Kill Devil Ridge onto the Lockett Range. Once onto the range the track tends southwards before the gradual descent into the Waingaro Valley. Water should be carried as the first major stream is not encountered until Skeet Creek, two-thirds of the way in from the road end. Waingaro Hut, which is also called Stanley Forks Hut (DOC, 4 bunks, open fire), is on a terrace between the Stanley and Waingaro Rivers. There are good campsites around the hut.

Cobb Valley

Longer tramps in the Cobb Valley begin at Trilobite Hut (DOC, 14 bunks, open fire) situated at the carpark at the southern end of the Cobb Reservoir. Also, from Myttons Hut (above the road shortly before Trilobite Hut), a track links the Cobb Valley with the Mt Arthur Tablelands.

Trilobite Hut (830 m) to Cobb Hut (1020 m) and Fenella Hut (1100 m): 3–4¹/₂ hours, Grade 2.

From Trilobite the track climbs gently up-valley, alternating through beech forests, open grasslands and occasional bogs. Chaffeys Hut, a disused wooden slab hut, is passed after 2 hours (Note: The bridge and track shown on the true right opposite Chaffeys on NZMS M26 no longer exists.) Beyond Chaffeys, crossing the Chaffey River is usually straightforward in normal flows but may be difficult in bad weather. Soon after, a stretch of boggy peatland must be tackled. A bridge (not marked on M26 or the Parkmap) takes the track to the true left shortly before Cobb Hut (DOC, 4 bunks, wood stove). An interesting side-trip from here is to Lake Cobb and Round Lake. Cobb Hut provides useful alternative accommodation and camping sites if the more attractive and popular Fenella Hut is full. Beyond the hut cross the footbridge north of Cobb Hut and climb up glaciated rock outcrops, past some spectacular foaming pools and waterfalls, to Fenella Hut (DOC, 20 bunks, open fire, gas cookers) below the beautiful Xenicus Peak. There is good camping near the hut, and plenty of scope for exploration from Fenella, including scrambles onto Mt Gibbs, west of the hut (fine views of Island Lake and the vast Tasman Wilderness Area), or up Kakapo Peak on the Snowden Range.

Fenella Hut (1100 m) to Lonely Lake Hut (1160 m) via the Douglas Range: 6–8 hours, Grade 3–4.

This is a route for experienced parties only, and not recommended in poor weather. From Fenella take the marked track heading northeast towards the Waingaro and Kakapo peaks. Initially the route climbs through forest on the true right of a creek draining Waingaro Peak. After gaining open ground, the route crosses the creek and continues to the peak's southern spur. Following cairns, the route (not poled as indicated in NZMS M26, Edition 1) sidles across the southeastern slopes of Waingaro Peak then gains the southern spur of Kakapo Peak. Either scramble onto and over Kakapo Peak, or alternatively bypass the summit by following a cairned route across its western slopes at about 1600 m. Continue along the Douglas Range until north of Point 1512. Here the track descends onto the western side of the range to avoid the next difficult section, then climbs back to the ridge south of Point 1610. Descend a rocky gully onto the eastern side of Point 1610 then traverse north to regain the ridge northeast of the peak. Staying on the ridge, the route descends to the bushline and falls gradually towards the glaciated cirque below the Drunken Sailors. Lonely Lake Hut (DOC, 3 bunks) is in this cirque on the edge of a stand of silver and mountain beech forest, and has good camping sites nearby.

Myttons Hut (910 m) to Balloon Hut (1250 m): 3–4 hours, Grade 3.

This is an alpine route to the Mt Arthur Tablelands. From Myttons, the track winds through forest to the Cobb Ridge where it meets the Cobb Ridge track. The track to Balloon Hut turns west and sidles towards the cirque containing Lake Peel. Turning southwards, the track continues onto the Peel Range and descends to Balloon Hut (DOC, 14 bunks, gas heating). See below for routes between Balloon Hut and Flora carpark. (A round trip back to the Cobb Reservoir is possible by descending Balloon Creek to the Upper Junction with the Takaka River, then continuing down the Takaka to the Lower Junction where the Bullock Track reaches the Takaka Valley. See page 41 for Bullock Track route description.)

Mount Arthur Tablelands

Flora carpark (960 m) to Salisbury Lodge (1130 m) via the Flora Track: 3–4 hours, Grade 2.

This is a popular and straightforward route along a wide, well-graded and benched track through scenic beech forests onto the Mt Arthur Tablelands. From Flora carpark follow the old four-wheel-drive road over Flora Saddle to Flora Hut (DOC, 12 bunks) 30 minutes from the road end. From here the track descends all the way to the Upper Junction where Flora Stream meets Balloon Creek. Here the track leaves the Flora Stream and begins a steady ascent to the tablelands, staying well above Balloon Creek on the true right. The forest edge is reached about $1^1/_2$ hours from the Upper Junction where signposts and poles lead across undulating tussock downs to the Salisbury Lodge (DOC, 24 bunks, gas cookers, wood stove), 20–30 minutes from the forest edge. This last section offers fine views of the western aspects of Mt Arthur and The Twins. Two large rock shelters along this route, one at Gridiron Gulch and the other signposted on the northern edge of the tablelands, provide superb alternative accommodation. They are both equipped with mattresses and open fireplaces.

Salisbury Lodge (1130 m) to Gordon's Pyramid (1489 m): 2 hours, Grade 2–3.

From the lodge head back towards Flora Hut for a few hundred metres to the signposted Gordon's Pyramid track turn-off. Follow poles east across the tablelands to where it enters the forest. The track through the forest is generally well marked, and after a short steep section emerges onto open ground. From here follow poles directly to Gordon's Pyramid, remembering to turn around to enjoy the views as they unfold behind you. (At the bushline an unmarked route follows the bush edge northeast to connect with the track to Clouston's Mine). From Gordon's Pyramid experienced parties can continue southeast on a poled route along Pyramid Ridge to Horseshoe Basin, and return to the Flora carpark down the Mt Arthur Track.

Salisbury Lodge (1130 m) to Balloon Hut (1250 m) via Starvation Ridge: 2 hours, Grade 2–3.

Follow the marked route behind the hut through increasingly stunted beech forest to Starvation Ridge. After about 30 minutes the track emerges onto open tussocklands and climbs gently to the junction with the Leslie Track. Soon after this junction the track descends to a forested saddle above Cundy Creek and turns northwards towards Balloon Hill. From here the track stays mostly on the tops, giving excellent views on a fine day. Balloon Hut (DOC, 14 bunks, gas) is reached shortly after Balloon Hill, nestled on the forest edge.

Salisbury Lodge (1130 m) to Karamea Bend Hut (370 m) via the Leslie Track: 5–6 hours, Grade 2.

From behind the lodge climb up the Balloon Track onto Starvation Ridge to the junction with the Leslie Track. From here it is a gradual descent into the Leslie Valley. Two huts are passed along the way: Splugeons Shelter (DOC, 10 bunks, open fire) after about 90 minutes, and Leslie Clearing (DOC, 6 bunks, open fire) 2–3 hours from Splugeons. Karamea Bend Hut (DOC, 12 bunks, open fire) is on a terrace above the junction of the Leslie and Karamea Rivers. See page 59 for information on the Karamea River.

Ellis and Baton Valleys

Both these valleys are reached from the Motueka Valley on the Baton Valley Road from Woodstock, on SH 61, about 35 km from Motueka. Each provides access onto the Mt Arthur Range. The Baton Valley begins at a ford 15 km from Woodstock, while the Ellis Valley starts about 1½ km further up the road. Both tracks are only irregularly maintained, and involve numerous river crossings.

Baton Ford to Flanagans Hut (1150 m): 5–6 hours, Grade 3–4.

The Baton track generally follows the route of an old benched pack track, now in disrepair, and is consequently in quite rough condition. The Baton must be crossed at least six times, several more crossings than indicated on map NZMS M27. From the ford, the track crosses farmland, and passes the Cowin track turn-off 300 m before a footbridge across the lower Baton. The track remains on the true left until two crossings are required before reaching the Loveridge track turnoff. There are three more crossings of the Baton beyond the Loveridge track before a longer stretch on the true right, then a final crossing

2 km from the hut. Continue to Flanagans Hut (DOC, 8 bunks, wood stove) which is located in forest in the upper Baton within sight of Baton Saddle.

Flanagans Hut to Baton Saddle (1360 m): 1–2 hours, Grade 3–4.
Continue up the valley, until the track emerges into subalpine scrub, notable for its profusion of spaniards. The track crosses the Baton again, now a small mountain stream, and follows standards up a steepening trail to the saddle. The saddle provides access to the tops along the southern end of the Mt Arthur Range. In good conditions, experienced parties can travel relatively easily along the tops towards Loveridge Spur, The Twins and Ellis Basin Hut. The range is exposed to bad weather. On the western side of the saddle, a track, sometimes overgrown and hard to follow, descends Wilkinson Creek into the Leslie Valley (see p. 54).

Side trips from the Baton Valley
Baton Ford to Mt Arthur Range via the Cowin Spur Track: 3–4 hours, Grade 2–3.
From the Baton ford, follow the Baton track as above to the Cowin Spur track junction. From here, the track up Cowin Spur can be quite overgrown and difficult to follow for the first hour of climbing. The steepness relents and continues through beech forest until the open tops are reached. In good conditions, ridge travel along the Mt Arthur Range is quite straightforward. Some parties use this route to provide access into the upper reaches of the untracked Crow River. Water should be carried.

Baton Ford to Mt Arthur tops via Loveridge Spur (1220 m): 4–5 hours, Grade 2–3.
Follow the Baton track as above to the junction with the Loveridge Spur Track, about 2–3 hours from Baton Ford. From above the western side of Loveridge Creek, a track climbs steeply through forest to the bush edge. (Note: Loveridge Hut has been removed.) The track may be overgrown at the start and difficult to find. From the treeline experienced parties will enjoy straightforward travel onto the Mt Arthur Range.

Ellis River Road (225 m) to Ellis Basin Hut (1110 m): 5–6 hours, Grade 3–4.
This is a difficult and poorly maintained and marked pack-track into the magnificent karst basin between Mt Arthur and The Twins. The track can be difficult to follow and involves many river crossings, dangerous in bad weather. From the road end stay on the true left until just past Hicky Clearing, where three crossings of the river are made in short succession. After the third, the track remains on the true right until just beyond a tributary that flows from the slopes of Barron Bold. Cross again, scramble up a rocky slope, then

sidle into and out of a gully, around a spur and descend to the river about 200 m upstream from Bruce Creek. A few hundred metres further on, a fork in the river is encountered. Cross the right branch above the fork, and continue for about a kilometre through a basin before crossing the river again. From here the track climbs steadily towards the hut. Ellis Basin Hut (DOC, 6 bunks) is the base for expeditions into the underground cave systems in Ellis Basin, and for attempts on The Twins. (Note: In good weather, the easiest route to Ellis Basin Hut is from the Mt Arthur Track, via a poled route that leads off from Winter Peak and descends into Ellis Basin.)

Wangapeka Valley

The Wangapeka Valley provides access to some superb tramping areas, the main interest to trampers being the Wangapeka Track. Mt Owen, the highest point in the park, amid impressive karst country, is also reached from the Wangapeka, via the Rolling River.

Access to the valley is from Tapawera in the Motueka Valley on SH 61. Following signposts from Tapawera, drive past the former Golden Downs Forest headquarters and turn right at Tadmor. Follow this road over Tadmor Saddle into the Wangapeka Valley. The Dart Ford may be impassable after heavy rain. Beyond the last homestead the road is subject to occasional washouts. An intentions book and telephone is located at an information kiosk shortly before the junction of the Rolling River and Wangapeka River, the beginning of the Wangapeka Track. To reach Mt Owen drive up the Rolling River and park at Courthouse Flat. There is a small 4-bunk hut at Rolling River Junction, and plenty of camping sites here and at Courthouse Flat.

WANGAPEKA TRACK

The Wangapeka Track is the second most popular tramping route in the park after the Heaphy. It links the Wangapeka Valley in the east with the Little Whanganui Valley in the west, the middle section passing through the headwaters of the Karamea River. This is an all weather route, though it is not as easy or as well-developed as the Heaphy, instead retaining the flavour of a good New Zealand back-country trail. It is usually walked in three or four days, and can be walked in either direction, although walking from east to west is easier because it avoids the long climb up Little Whanganui Saddle. The track is well serviced by huts of varying standards, and there are numerous camping sites.

Rolling Junction Hut (300 m) to Kings Creek Hut (560 m): 3–4 hours, Grade 2.

From Rolling Junction Hut (DOC, 4 bunks, campsites) cross the swingbridge over the Rolling River and head west up the true right bank of the Wangapeka River. Initially the track crosses open scrubby flats, then enters beech forest. Splendid views of Mt Patriarch are a highlight of the walk. The track crosses to the true left about 20–30 minutes from Kings Creek Hut, at the junction of Kiwi Stream and the Wangapeka River. Kings Creek Hut (DOC, 30 bunks, gas cookers, wood stove), is located in a large clearing above the river.

Kings Creek Hut (560 m) to Stone Hut (660 m): 2–3 hours, Grade 2.
A few minutes from Kings Creek Hut, the track passes Kings Hut, an old slab hut dating to the 1930s recently restored by DOC, and worth a stay for those interested in a rustic camping experience. A few minutes further upstream the Wangapeka River forks and the track continues up the true left of the Wangapeka's north branch. Shortly after Luna Stream, the track crosses to the true right. Stone Hut (DOC, 12 bunks, gas cookers) is 30 minutes from the crossing opposite Stone Creek.

Stone Hut (660 m) to Helicopter Flat Hut (720 m) via Wangapeka Saddle (1000 m): 3–5 hours, Grade 2.
Not far from Stone Hut the track crosses a large earthquake slip (that came down in the 1929 Murchison earthquake), then zigzags through forest to Wangapeka Saddle. From the saddle, the track descends into the headwaters of the Karamea River. Cross the Karamea (straightforward in normal flows; 3-wire walkwire, 100 m upstream when river is in flood) and then continue along the true left for about an hour, when the track crosses again to the true right. The river is recrossed 30 minutes later on, and then continues to Helicopter Flat. A high level route avoids these last two crossings if the river is high, but adds 20 minutes to this section. Helicopter Flat Hut (DOC, 12 bunks, gas cookers) lies a few minutes from Waters Creek.

Helicopter Flat Hut (720 m) to Taipo Hut (680 m): 3–4 hours, Grade 2.
Staying on the true right, the track passes Brough's Tabernacle (above the junction of the Karamea and Taipo Rivers), then crosses a ridge and moves into the Taipo Valley. A swingbridge takes the track to the true left of the Taipo River. The Karamea Track (see p. 59) turns right, while the Wangapeka continues up the Taipo, climbing steadily to Taipo Hut (DOC, 18 bunks, gas cookers).

Taipo Hut (680 m) to Little Whanganui Hut (300 m) via Little Whanganui Saddle (1100 m): 5–7 hours, Grade 2.
From Taipo Hut, the track climbs steadily to the open tops of Little Whanganui Saddle, passing the turn-off to the rundown Stag Flat Hut (DOC, 4 bunks) before the final climb to the saddle. With tarns and fine views to the West Coast, the saddle is a place worth lingering at on a good day. It's a long 450 m descent from the saddle into the Little Whanganui Valley. At the bottom the track crosses a footbridge onto the true right of the river. The gorge below

Tangent Creek, one hour from the bridge, can be tackled by crossing to the true left and boulder-hopping downriver. Watch closely for the cairn indicating where to rejoin the track on the true right. If the river is too high for this option, a wet weather alternative climbs steeply around the gorge and rejoins the track at Smith Creek. A swingbridge 15 minutes from Smith Creek leads to Little Whanganui (or Belltown) Hut (DOC, 16 bunks, gas cookers) on a terrace above the true left bank of the river.

Little Whanganui Hut (300 m) to road end: 3–4 hours, Grade 2.

Cross back over the swingbridge to the true right of the river. The fastest route to the road end is down the riverflats following marker poles and fording the river where required. A longer wet weather alternative continues along the true right, past Gilmore Clearing, then along an old logging road to the road end.

Side trips in the Wangapeka Valley

Wangapeka Valley (400 m) to Kiwi Saddle Hut (1020 m): 2–3 hours, Grade 2–3.

The track to Kiwi Saddle begins at the bridge 30 minutes downstream from Kings Creek Hut. Ford Kiwi Stream (difficult in high flows) then climb steadily along a benched track on the true left of the stream. Kiwi Saddle Hut (DOC 6 bunks, wood stove) is on the bush edge on Kiwi Saddle, below Mt Patriarch. In good conditions it is possible to traverse west to Mt Luna and descend to the Wangapeka Valley via the Stone Track (see below). Experienced parties can take the track into the Taylor Valley, beyond which lies unmarked territory down the Crow Valley. Mt Patriarch can be climbed in good weather, and a traverse of the mountain is possible by descending back into the Wangapeka Valley down Gibbs Track, or down Chummies Track from John Reid Hut. The traverse should only be attempted in good weather and by those experienced at routefinding in alpine areas. The Gomorrah Track marked on topomaps is no longer maintained.

Stone Hut (760 m) to Mt Luna (1630 m) via the Stone Track: 3–4 hours, Grade 3.

From Stone Hut, ford the Wangapeka River and pick up the marked track that climbs through forest on the true left of Stone Creek. About one kilometre up the creek the track crosses to the true right, and continues to the bush edge. There is an excellent campsite on the forest edge at the head of the creek. Climb tussock slopes to Mt Luna's southern ridge and scramble to the summit, a splendid viewpoint over the Karamea and Wangapeka valleys, and of Mt Kendall and Mt Patriarch. (The unmarked route to Kiwi Saddle sidles beneath Point 1578, south of Mt Luna, then follows the ridge heading east to the

Saddle.) Mt Luna, and the traverse to Kiwi Saddle, should only be undertaken in good weather and by experienced parties.

Wangapeka Saddle (1000 m) to the Biggs Tops (1384 m): 1 hour to bush-edge, Grade 2–3.

From Wangapeka Saddle take the track that tends northwest up a forest-covered ridge. Once on the tops, it's a straightforward (in good weather) trek along a ridge that curls westwards to Biggs Tops which overlooks the upper Karamea catchment. A route marked on NZMS 260 M28 that descends from the Biggs Tops to the Karamea Valley is steep, overgrown, difficult to follow and not recommended.

Karamea Valley

Trampers are slowly discovering the Karamea Valley, savouring its remoteness and beauty. The Karamea Track is generally well marked and bridged from its headwaters in the south to Karamea Bend. The main tramping routes into the Karamea Valley are the Wangapeka Track or down the Leslie Track (for Leslie Track approach, see page 54) from the Mt Arthur Tablelands. From the Motueka Valley, the loop joining the Wangapeka, Karamea, Leslie and Mt Arthur Tablelands tracks is an increasingly popular 5–7 day tramp of some 90–100 km duration. Access is from the Wangapeka Track.

Helicopter Flat Hut (720 m) to Luna Hut/Trevor Carter Hut (500 m) via Lost Valley Track: 1¹/₂–2 hours, Grade 2.

From the hut head downstream a few minutes, to Waters Creek. Ford the Karamea River and pick up the marked track that leads to Lost Valley Saddle. The saddle is reached in about 20 minutes, next to a small forest-fringed tarn. From here down Lost Valley, take the best-looking route down the creek until about two-thirds of the way down where the track moves to the true right all the way to Luna Hut. You will see an impressive series of earthquake scars on the slopes of Biggs Tops. Luna Hut (DOC, 4 bunks, fireplace) is 15 minutes downstream from Trevor Carter Hut (DOC, 6 bunks, fireplace), which is located on the true left bank of the Karamea. In normal flows crossing the Karamea is straightforward.

Brough's Tabernacle (680 m) to Trevor Carter/Luna Huts (500 m): 1 hour, Grade 2.

Take the track leading down to the Karamea River. About 200 m from the Taipo/Karamea confluence, a track branches off to Luna Hut, crossing the Karamea and moving down the true right. If continuing on to Trevor Carter Hut, cross the Taipo just above the confluence and find the track from the Taipo footbridge on the true left, a few minutes from the hut, below the Luna Slips.

Taipo River footbridge (570 m) to Trevor Carter Hut (500 m): 30 minutes, Grade 1.

This is the start of the Karamea Track and the safest route from the Wangapeka Track to Trevor Carter Hut because it avoids the need to ford the Karamea River. From the bridge it is a straightforward walk to the hut (DOC, 6 bunks, fireplace) on the true left.

Trevor Carter Hut (500 m) to Thor Hut (530 m): 3–4 hours, Grade 2.

Staying on the true left, the track crosses Kendall Creek (unbridged, and can be impassable during storms), then continues through forested riverflats towards Moonstone Lake, a lake formed by slips loosed by the 1929 Murchison earthquake. The side creeks from here till Crow Hut have been imaginatively named after Greek gods. Thor Hut (DOC, 6 bunks, fireplace) is a pleasant place for a lunch stop if you have started your day from Trevor Carter.

Thor Hut (530 m) to Venus Hut (370 m): 2–3 hours, Grade 2.

Keeping on the true left, the track proceeds through splendid beech forest, then climbs over bluffs near Atlas Creek, giving good views of the river. The next major creek, Mercury Creek, is bridged, and from there it's about half an hour to the wonderfully located two-storey Venus Hut (DOC, 12 bunks), high above the river on a rocky knob.

Venus Hut (370 m) to Crow Hut (307 m): 2–3 hours, Grade 2.

Cross the footbridge over Venus Creek and continue for about an hour (Jupiter Creek is also bridged) to a swingbridge that takes the track to the true right. The track then climbs briefly, follows an old watercourse back to the main river and carries on to Crow Hut (DOC, 6 bunks, fireplace) at the confluence of the Crow and Karamea Rivers.

Crow Hut (307 m) to Karamea Bend Hut (264 m): 3–4 hours, Grade 2.

The next section of track affords excellent views of the limestone bluffs of Garibaldi Ridge. Cross the bridge over the Crow and begin the straightforward tramp along forested and open riverflats, with increasingly better views of the impressive limestone formations in the area, all the way to the Bend. At the Bend, pass the DOC staff quarters on a terrace above the river, and continue to the Leslie/Karamea confluence. A short way up the Leslie lies Karamea Bend Hut (DOC, 12 bunks, fireplace).

OTHER ROUTES

The route marked on topomaps from the Taipo Valley to Kakapo Saddle via Herbert Creek has been closed by DOC.

Little Whanganui Valley to Kakapo Hut via the Kakapo Track: 6–7 hours, Grade 2–3.

This is a rough track which leaves the Wangapeka Track at Drain Creek, about

10 minutes downstream from Little Whanganui Hut. The first section of track to Lawrence Saddle is in relatively good condition, but from here on the route becomes overgrown. Whether or not this track remains open will depend on DOC maintenance priorities.

Mount Owen — northern approaches from Courthouse Flat
Courthouse Flat (360 m) to Granity Pass Hut (1200 m) via Billies Knob Track: 5–6 hours, Grade 2.

Water should be carried as there is little to be obtained on this route. From Courthouse Flat the most common route is to follow the track up the ridge between Granity and Blue Creeks, though an alternative start is to follow up Blue Creek and climb steeply up through forest to gain the ridge-top track. The ridge track climbs through regenerating scrub, beech forest and occasional open clearings to Billies Saddle. (From the saddle it's possible to clamber along the ridge to Billies Knob for panoramic views, including Mt Patriarch above the Wangapeka Valley.) The track descends steeply into Blue Creek, continues in forest past a dilapidated slab hut (Taplins Shelter) before emerging into the subalpine scrub at the head of the valley. From here the track follows up a dry creek bed to the entrance of Ghost Valley and Granity Pass Hut (DOC, 6 bunks, wood stove, gas cookers) on a terrace above the true right of the stream. There are good camping sites in the vicinity of the hut or further east in Sanctuary Basin.

Granity Pass Hut (1200 m) to Mt Owen (1875 m): 3 hours, Grade 2–3.

From the hut there is a popular day excursion to Mt Owen, the highest peak in the park, through intriguing glaciated marble landscape. Cross to the 'Railway Embankment' (actually an old glacial moraine) opposite the hut and follow cairns east into Sanctuary Basin, then north around Sentinel Hill towards Mt Owen. There are numerous potential camping sites in the meadows below Mt Owen, and many tarns. Find your own route through the marble outcrops on the final climb to the trig, but take good care. The route will be difficult to follow in misty or bad weather.

Courthouse Flat (360 m) to Granity Pass Hut (1200 m) via Cullifords Hill (1756 m): 5–6 hours, Grade 2–4.

This is an alternative route to Granity Pass, often used as a descent route in a round trip from the Billies Knob Track. It should be attempted only in good weather by experienced parties. From Courthouse Flat head to Blue Creek, cross the Blue Creek footbridge and move up Cullifords Track on the ridge between Blue and Nuggety Creeks. The first 2 km of track may be overgrown with gorse, bracken and fern, making it difficult and/or painful to follow. The track is easier to follow once forest is reached. Higher up, the Nuggety Creek

Track is signposted leading back into Nuggety Creek. The bushline is reached soon after the junction and from here pick the best route through marble outcrops to Point 1597. Descend to a tussock saddle and continue along the ridge towards Cullifords Hill. Difficult sections of ridge can be avoided on the western side. The best route from Cullifords Hill to Granity Pass Hut is to descend the spur heading southwest from the Cullifords Hill Trig, across a saddle and proceed south to a second saddle below Point 1552. From here descend west in Sanctuary Basin to pick up the path on the prominent 'Railway Embankment' that descends into Ghost Valley.

Mount Owen — southern approaches

The southern access to Mt Owen is along the Owen Valley Road from the Buller Gorge on SH 6, near the Owen River Hotel. Permission will be required from landowners to camp at the road end. Contact DOC for details.

Owen Valley (370 m) to Mt Owen (1875 m) via Sunset Ridge: 6–7 hours, Grade 2–4.

Follow DOC signposts to the start of the Sunset Ridge track, 16 km from SH 6. The route, an old pack-track, stays on the true left of the Owen River for 2 km, then four crossings are made in quick succession close to Bulmer Creek. (An unofficial caver's track leads up Bulmer Creek to a campsite next to Lake Bulmer.) Shortly after Bulmer Creek the track to Sunset Ridge begins climbing a steep ridge towards the bushline. Scramble up tussocks to the ridge below Sunrise Peak. Continue northwards over the peak towards Mt Owen, taking the best route through the marble formations. The Mt Owen trig is at the eastern end of the peak's summit ridge. This alpine section of the route should be undertaken only in good weather. Experienced parties could descend to Granity Pass Hut, or head northwest over Replica Hill to Point 1500, then descend north to pick up the start of the track leading to Branch Creek Hut.

Owen Valley (370 m) to Branch Creek Hut (940 m) via the Fyffe Valley: 5–6 hours, Grade 2.

Permission must be sought from the landowner to reach the valley. Contact DOC for details and directions for reaching the Fyffe River. A signpost on the western side of the Fyffe River marks the start of the track which begins along a farm track on the true right of Frying Pan Creek. At the saddle between Frying Pan and Sandstone Creeks the recommended option is to climb directly into the Fyffe Valley (the Sandstone Creek track is difficult and poorly marked). Once in the Fyffe the route is obvious and the many crossings of the river are straightforward in normal flows. Beyond Branch Creek Hut (DOC, 6 bunks, fireplace), tracks lead into the headwaters of the Fyffe and up to Replica Hill. If descending the Fyffe, stay at the bush edge when approaching the lower gorge section, as the track leading over to Frying Pan Creek can be easily missed.

Matiri Valley

At the southern end of the park, the Matiri Valley is neglected by many trampers, though it is one of the finest areas in the park. Most people venture onto the magnificent 100 Acre and 1000 Acre Plateaux, two of the oldest ancient geological formations in New Zealand. The tramp to the headwaters of the Matiri is also worthwhile for its forests, lakes and dramatic earthquake slips.

MATIRI VALLEY TRACK

Lake Matiri (343 m) to McConchies Hut (450 m): 3–4 hours, Grade 2.
See page 44 for a description of the track to Lake Matiri. Head round the western side of Lake Matiri, cross Bay Creek past the 100 Acre Plateau track junction and continue along open, scrubby river flats beyond the lake. The track stays on the true right of the Matiri, passing a number of camping sites along the way and occasionally taking to the forest or over slips. McConchies Hut (DOC, 6 bunks, open fire) is on the edge of a clearing above the Matiri River.

McConchies Hut (450 m) to Hurricane Hut (810 m): 6–7 hours, Grade 2.
Continuing along the west bank of the Matiri, this section of track is rougher and not as well marked in places. Care should be taken where the track leaves the Matiri River at the second (unnamed) major side valley encountered about 90 minutes from the hut. The track moves up this valley through fallen boulders and is marked only with cairns and occasional painted markers on rocks. Twenty minutes up, the track climbs onto the ridge between the side valley and the Matiri, crosses a slip and continues more easily up the ridge for about 2 km. There are good views of Lake Bradley, an earthquake lake, as the track proceeds through some excellent mixed beech, podocarp and dracophyllum forest. Where the ridge broadens, the track descends west to a clearing in the upper reaches of the unnamed creek and goes over a small rise to another small clearing. Soon after, the track swings eastwards and rejoins the Matiri Valley. Hurricane Hut (DOC, 4 bunks, open fire) is about 40 minutes beyond Lake Jeanette.

MATIRI RANGE (100 ACRE AND 1000 ACRE PLATEAUX)

Lake Matiri (343 m) to Poor Pete's Hut (1060 m): 2–3 hours, Grade 2.
Take the track round the western side of the lake to Bay Creek. On the

northern side of the creek the track to Poor Pete's Hut is signposted at the foot of a spur. From here it's a long and steep haul through beech forest to the edge of the 1000 Acre Plateau. There are a number of vantage points along the way offering a pause for breath and views of dramatic limestone cliffs and Lake Matiri. About halfway there is a brief respite from the climb but the track soon steepens again. Trees thin towards the edge of the plateau before giving way to open tussock boglands. Follow the poled route north across the plateau to Poor Pete's Hut (DOC, 2 bunks, open fire) which despite its poor condition is still usable. There are camping sites near the hut.

Poor Pete's Hut (1060 m) to Larrikins Hut (1050 m): 3–4 hours, Grade 2–3.

In good weather this is a straightforward tramp following a poled route along the broad and boggy tops of the Matiri Range. The track climbs the slope above Poor Pete's to Pt 1115 then gradually descends to Larrikins Creek. The route is often boggy underfoot, and passes numerous tarns and streams. There are increasingly better views west to the craggy edges of the 100 Acre Plateau, and down Larrikins Creek into the Mokihinui Valley. Just over 1 km from Larrikins Hut the track re-enters the forest. Larrikins Hut (DOC, 4 bunks, open fire) is nestled on the edge of a clearing which offers good camping. Although not marked on the NZMS M28, there is a route that leads northwest towards the 100 Acre Plateau and The Needle, a splendid viewpoint. From The Needle it is a relatively easy scramble along the ridge towards The Haystack.

nelson lakes *national park*

Rising in Fiordland, the Southern Alps extend in an unbroken line up the South Island until, dwindling in height, they merge into the ranges south of Nelson. Here at the northern end of the Alps, centred around two tranquil mountain lakes, lies the Nelson Lakes National Park. Lake Rotoiti and Lake Rotoroa, framed by mountains and with forest creeping down to their edges, are on the northern fringes of the park, with a tangle of remote valleys and mountains to the south forming its heart.

The great Alpine Fault of the South Island dissects the park. At 650 km long, it marks the edges of two huge plates in the earth's crust. The fault runs across the head of Lake Rotoroa and cuts through the peninsula between Kerr Bay and West Bay on Lake Rotoiti. On its northwestern side lies granite about 300 million years old, completely different from the younger sedimentary rocks found on the southern side of the fault. In the last 10 million years this granite has moved some 480 km along the fault after splitting from that still found in Fiordland. The granite country is much lower than that to the south of the fault, where buckled and shattered greywacke and sandstone mountains have been pushed upwards. Until about 12,000 years ago successive ice ages ravaged this region. Massive glaciers carved out the valleys, gouging especially deep holes in the Travers, Sabine and D'Urville Valleys which are now filled by the two lakes.

About 8000 years ago when the glacial ice retreated, beech forest slowly spread back into the park to become the predominant forest type, although some stands of podocarp forest are found on river flats and lake fringes. A very ancient forest type, beech forest supports a wide diversity of other life. Most obvious are the birds. With relatively little nectar, berries or flowers to feed on in the beech forest, insect-feeding birds are most common: the robin, fantail, tomtit, grey warbler, rifleman, as well as the bellbird and tui. At about 1400 m the conditions become too harsh for beech trees to survive and the forest gives way to fields of snow tussock, alpine herbs, scree and rock.

Nelson Lakes is part of the Maori world. Their myth tells of a great chief

Rakaihaitu who, when he reached the area, seized his great ko, or digging stick, and dug the huge holes now known as Rotoiti and Rotoroa. His task completed, Rakaihaitu journeyed further south, digging and naming all the great southern lakes. The park never seems to have been settled by the Maori people, though the lakes, with their abundant supply of eels and mussels, were popular stopping-off points on the route between Tasman Bay, the West Coast and Canterbury. Midden sites in the Travers Valley, Kerr Bay and in the Matakitaki Valley, and a fern garden above Rotoroa are all evidence of Maori visits.

When John Cotterell, a surveyor in search of flat land for farming, stumbled upon Lake Rotoiti in 1843 with his companion Dick Peanter there were no Maori living there. They were the first Europeans to find what is now the park and were followed three years later by the Maori guide Kehu who brought Charles Heaphy, William Fox and Thomas Brunner to the shores of Lake Rotoroa. By 1848 the Rotoiti sheep run had been established. In the next 10 years exploration continued with a visit by the German geologist and naturalist Julius Von Haast, and later by an inspired Nelson solicitor, William Travers, who ventured into much of the back country. The discovery of gold on the West Coast in the 1860s prompted the upgrading of the track between Nelson and the Coast, thereby establishing reasonable access to the fringes of the park.

After his visit, Haast commented in 1860 that 'I am sure that the time is not far distant when this spot will become the favourite abode and resort of those whose means and leisure will permit them to admire picturesque and magnificent scenery'. His was a far-sighted vision. Though relatively few came to appreciate the area in the years that followed his visit, the arrival of the motor car in the 1930s saw the beginning of the development of St Arnaud, in recognition of the scenic and recreational value of the area. In 1956 an area of 140,000 acres was gazetted as Nelson Lakes National Park, and the boundaries of the park were extended in 1983 to include the Spenser Mountains and the Matakitaki and Glenroy Valleys.

Nelson Lakes is very accessible to trampers. Though the higher peaks in the park rise well above 2000 m, when compared with the high Alps further south the country is relatively gentle. Tracks wind up most of the bushclad valleys and in good summer conditions the many routes crossing passes and ridges are within the capabilities of most trampers. For an alpine area the park has a relatively moderate climate, often enjoying long periods of settled weather. Nelson Lakes National Park offers much of the magnificence and isolation of New Zealand's mountain areas, but does so without the demands and challenges found elsewhere.

Information

PARK VISITOR CENTRE AND AREA OFFICE

The Nelson Lakes National Park Area Office is at St Arnaud. The DOC Area Office incorporates a visitor centre with the usual information and services, as well as informative textual and audio-visual displays. The visitor centre is generally open from 8.00 a.m. until 4.30 p.m. seven days a week, though is open later during the summer season.

> St Arnaud Area Office
> Department of Conservation
> PO Box 55
> St Arnaud
> Phone (03) 521 1806
> Fax (03) 521 1896

Intentions can be recorded here and up to date weather and track information is available.

ACCESS

From Blenheim SH 63 leads straight up the Wairau Valley to St Arnaud. From Nelson two routes are commonly used. The first turns off SH 6 at Belgrove south of Nelson. Drive up the Wai-iti Valley and then follow a sealed road through Golden Downs State Forest to join the Korere-Tophouse Road. The second route leaves SH 6 further south of Nelson at Korere to pick up the road through Tophouse to St Arnaud. When travelling north from Murchison on SH 6, turn off at Kawatiri Junction and follow SH 63 to reach St Arnaud. Lake Rotoroa is reached via the Gowan River Road, which turns off SH 63 south of Kawatiri Junction at Gowan Bridge. To reach the Matakitaki boundary of the park follow the Tutaki Road which turns off SH 6 just north of Murchison, and the Matakitaki Road leading directly south out of Murchison through Six Mile leads to the Glenroy Valley and the western boundary of the park.

TRANSPORT SERVICES

Wadsworth Motors, based in Tapawera (phone (03) 522 4248), operate a return bus service on Monday, Wednesday and Friday between St Arnaud and Nelson. Nelson Lakes Shuttles (phone (03) 521 1887) offers an on-demand shuttle service to road ends in the park. White Star operate buses on SH 6 between Nelson and Christchurch, while Intercity operates on SH 6 between Nelson and the West Coast. There is a water taxi available by arrangement on both Lakes Rotoiti (phone (03) 521 1894) and Rotoroa (phone (03) 523 9199).

ACCOMMODATION

Camping grounds: The park has three camping grounds. At Lake Rotoiti the camping ground at Kerr Bay has a shelter, an amenity building with showers, toilets, a washing machine and disabled toilet and shower, as well as powered camp sites. At West Bay there are toilets, showers, a kitchen with cookers and powered camp sites. Bookings for both grounds can be made at the visitor centre. At Lake Rotoroa there is a self-registration camping ground with toilets and water taps. No bookings are taken and there is a small charge.

Hostels and lodges: There are two backpacker lodges at St Arnaud, while Rotoiti Lodge is a large educational resource centre at St Arnaud, with bunk accommodation for 76. Bookings can be made by phoning (03) 521 1820. Red Deer Lodge at St Arnaud has 28 bunks and is operated by the Nelson branch of the NZ Deerstalkers Association. Phone (03) 521 1800 for bookings.

Motels and hotels: At St Arnaud there is the Alpine Lodge hotel, self-contained Log Chalets, holiday homes available through the shop, and bed and breakfast accommodation at Tophouse. At Rotoroa there is the exclusive Lake Rotoroa Guesthouse.

SERVICES

The Lake Rotoiti Service Centre at St Arnaud is open seven days a week and offers petrol, public telephone, a postal agency on weekdays, groceries and takeaway food. There are no shops at Lake Rotoroa.

WEATHER

As the park is protected by ranges to the west, south and east, the intensity and frequency of bad weather is reduced in this area in comparison to other parts of the Southern Alps. The park is often blessed with periods of fine weather, most common in summer, early autumn and winter. Most rain comes from prevailing north and south westerlies off the Tasman Sea, and there is more precipitation in the west than in the east. Snow generally lies above the bushline for much of winter, regularly falling in the valleys below.

MAPS

Parkmap 273/05 of Nelson Lakes National Park covers all of the park and has huts and tracks marked. For more detailed information trampers should use the Topomap 260 series, in particular N29 St Arnaud, M29 Murchison, M30 Matakitaki and N30 Tarndale.

FURTHER READING

The park handbook *The Story of Nelson Lakes National Park* (DOC/Cobb Horwood, 1984) gives the best insight into the natural and social history and recreational values of the park. DOC have published a number of booklets and pamphlets on subjects related to the park, including a series of sheets with tramping information.

Short walks

WALKS AROUND LAKE ROTOITI

The Peninsula Nature Walk: 1¹/₂–3 hours return, Grade 1, pamphlet available.

This gentle nature walk meanders around the forested peninsula that juts out into Lake Rotoiti. The walk starts from the western end of Kerr Bay, and for those wanting to return to St Arnaud eventually crosses back over the peninsula to View Road. Alternatively, you can follow the track around the shores of the lake to West Bay.

Black Valley Walk: 30 minutes, Grade 1.

This easy walk begins in Kerr Bay and follows the Black Valley Stream up through beech forest to SH 63 in the St Arnaud village.

Black Hill Walk: 1¹/₂ hours return, Grade 1.

Black Hill, rising to the north of Rotoiti Lodge, is a knob of hard volcanic rock shaped by ancient glaciers. The track begins at Rotoiti Lodge and zigzags through groves of kanuka and manuka trees to the summit 127 m above the lake. The odd beech tree is all that remains of the original forest, destroyed by fire earlier this century. From the top you can return as you came, or continue down the steeper northern side and walk back on the track that runs beside SH 63.

Moraine Walk: 1¹/₂ hours return, Grade 1.

The Moraine Walk starts off the highway 1 km west of St Arnaud where the track up the northern side of Black Hill begins. It traverses above West Bay across terminal moraine deposited during the last glaciation. Initially skirting Black Hill, the track crosses the West Bay Road and stays on a moraine ridge until reaching the Buller River. Along the way the track passes two kettle ponds that were formed when glacial ice failed to drain away. The track also gives views across the lake and out to the north across the head of the Buller Valley.

Anglers' Walk: 1 hour return, Grade 1.

The Buller River starts its long journey to the West Coast at West Bay on Lake Rotoiti. Beginning just down from the river's source on the edge of the West

Bay camping ground, the Anglers' Walk follows the river for a small section of its course, ending at the first bridge over the Buller on SH 63.

Loop Track: 1¹/₂ hours return, Grade 1–2.

The Loop Track offers an easy walk in the beech forest above Lake Rotoiti. It initially follows the St Arnaud Ridge Walk which branches off the Lakehead Track near its beginning at Kerr Bay. After climbing gradually upwards for half an hour on the St Arnaud Ridge Walk, the Loop Track leaves this walk and circles back down through tall forest to the lake shore. Here it rejoins the Lakehead Track and returns to Kerr Bay.

Mt Robert Ridge Walk: 5 hours return, Grade 2.

Mt Robert, with its eroding face clearly obvious from St Arnaud, has two well-worn tracks to its ridge. For those equipped for some walking on the tops these can be linked together to give a fine day's outing. Both tracks begin at the Mt Robert carpark at the end of the road which gives access to West Bay. The longer way to the bushline is via Paddy's Track, which begins at the bend in the road immediately below the carpark. This track sweeps across the face of Mt Robert and climbs to Bushline Hut (DOC, 16 bunks, wood and coal stove) perched high above the lake on the eastern end of Mt Robert. From here you can follow a poled trail on open tops around a gentle cirque to meet the Pinchgut Track and the Mt Robert Ridge.

The Pinchgut Track is an easier way to gain the ridge. It begins at the carpark and zigzags up open slopes and through beech forest to a shelter on the bush edge. Relax Shelter is a further 15 minutes from here on the ridge proper, where fine views warrant the effort. If you want to make a round trip, the route to Bushline Hut and Paddy's Track leaves the ridge just above Relax Shelter. In good conditions the poles on the Robert Ridge can be followed up to an observation shelter above the skifield in Second Basin.

St Arnaud Ridge Walk: 5 hours return, Grade 3, pamphlet available.

Suitable for the more energetic, this walk leads from the lake to the crest of the St Arnaud Range. The track branches off the Lakehead Track near its beginning at the eastern end of Kerr Bay. After climbing over a series of gentle glacial terraces, it begins a steeper but gradual climb up a spur to the bush edge and the Parachute Rocks. From here, in snow-free conditions, you can follow directly up the slopes to the ridgeline for expansive views in all directions.

Rotoiti Lakehead Track: 6–9 hours return or round trip, Grade 1.

Two picturesque and undulating tracks give access up both sides of Lake Rotoiti, and the trip to the lake head up one side with a return by the other makes a pleasant day trip. To make the round trip a crossing of the Travers River is required at the head of the lake. This is normally only a knee-deep ford but must not be undertaken if the river is up. If the river is not fordable it is

possible to continue up-valley for 1¹/₂ hours to a swingbridge over the river —
allow 9 hours for the total circuit if using this swingbridge. The track on the
eastern side of the lake begins at the east end of Kerr Bay and winds in and
out of many little bays to reach Lakehead Hut (DOC, 36 bunks, wood/coal
stove) just past the actual head of the lake. Ford the Travers River directly out
from the hut and a track on the far bank leads across the valley and down to
Coldwater Hut (DOC, 6 bunks, open fire) on the shore of the lake. The track
around the western shores of the lake begins by the hut, passes the site of an
old illicit still at Whiskey Falls and eventually comes out on the road to the Mt
Robert carpark, up from West Bay.

WALKS AROUND LAKE ROTOROA

There is a pamphlet available with information about these walks.

Flowers Walk: 5–10 minutes return, Grade 1.

This short bush walk bears the name of two early settlers at Lake Rotoroa,
Hubert and Cyril Flower. It begins to the right of the carpark on the lake shore,
and, skirting the lake outlet, travels through a rare tall stand of kahikatea forest.

Short Loop Track: 20 minutes return, Grade 1.

An especially good track for anyone interested in the botany of the area, this
track can be found at the northern end of the picnic area on the lake shore.
The track follows the Lakeside Track for 10 minutes before circling back to the
beginning of the Porika Track through a diverse forest of beech and podocarp
trees.

**Porika Lookout Track: 1¹/₂ hours return for shorter option, 2¹/₂ hours
return for longer option, Grade 1.**

On the northern end of the Muntz Range above Lake Rotoroa, the Porika
Lookout gives impressive views down the full length of the lake to the
mountains at its head. By taking a left turn on the road at the Rotoroa
Guesthouse you will arrive at a carpark and the beginning of the two routes
to the Porika Lookout. For the easier and shorter option follow the four-wheel-
drive track (which services the power lines crossing the range) to the lookout,
taking around 40 minutes. A more interesting, though longer, option is to
follow the old Porika Stock Track, which branches off the four-wheel-drive
track after 15 minutes' walking from the carpark. Climb up this track through
an area of regenerating forest to the four-wheel-drive track, where a walk
back down the track leads to the lookout and eventually the carpark.

The Braeburn Walk: 1¹/₂–2 hours return, Grade 1.

Beginning 100 m up the road from the Rotoroa bridge, this easy walk takes
you first into the heart of a fine area of beech/podocarp forest, and then to a
graceful waterfall. Initially travelling on the wide remains of a road used for

hydro-electric investigations in the 1950s, the track branches off the road after 10–15 minutes and gradually climbs to reach the Braeburn Waterfall. For a round trip from here follow down the track alongside the stream to the flats and the old road, where a left turn will lead back to your starting point.

Tramping trip summary

The following summary outlines most of the recognised tramping trips undertaken in Nelson Lakes National Park. Used with the route descriptions that follow, it can provide a basis for planning a tramp. Remember, however, that these are only suggestions and by using a map and consulting DOC staff many variations on these tramps can be found. The times given make no allowance for delays caused by bad weather.

- Beginning at St Arnaud, Travers Valley to Sabine Valley via Travers Saddle. Down Sabine Valley to head of Lake Rotoroa (4 days). For a visit to Blue Lake in West Sabine Valley add 1 day. From head of Lake Rotoroa walk to bottom of lake and road end (1 day) or use water taxi. Alternatively, return to St Arnaud via the Howard/Speargrass track (1–2 days) or via Mt Cedric, Lake Angelus and either Robert Ridge or Travers Valley (2 days).
- Beginning at Mt Robert carpark, to Lake Angelus via Robert Ridge. Return via same route, or via Hukere Stream and Travers Valley (2 days). Alternatively continue from Lake Angelus to Hopeless Creek via Sunset Saddle (1 day). (This is an unmarked route.)
- Beginning at St Arnaud, Travers Valley to Hopeless Creek and return via same route (2 days).
- Beginning at St Arnaud, Travers Valley to Cupola Hut and return via same route (2–3 days).
- Beginning at head of Lake Rotoroa, up Sabine Valley to Blue Lake, to D'Urville Valley via Moss Pass, and down D'Urville Valley to head of Lake Rotoroa (4–5 days).
- Beginning at Tutaki Road end, up Matakitaki Valley to forks, up East Matakitaki Valley to D'Urville Valley via David Saddle, down D'Urville Valley and return to starting point via Mole Saddle or Tiraumea Valley (5 days).
- Beginning at Tutaki Road end, up Matakitaki Valley to forks, up West Matakitaki Valley to Glenroy Valley via unnamed pass, down Glenroy Valley to road end (5 days).

Tramping

THE TRAVERS VALLEY

Running from the head of Lake Rotoiti back into the mountains, the Travers Valley is accessible and popular. With good tracks in the main valley and up a number of side valleys, bridges over all major rivers and streams, and numerous huts, it is fine tramping country.

Rotoiti Lakehead (630 m) to John Tait Hut (820 m) via Travers Valley: 5 hours, Grade 2.

The lower reaches of the Travers Valley are particularly attractive, with regular grassy flats fringed by forest. For tracks to the head of Lake Rotoiti see page 71. Above the lake head you can choose between tracks on either side of the valley with little difference in time and effort between them. On the eastern side of the river pick up the track from Lakehead Hut, which gives mostly easy travel over open flats and through forest to a swingbridge over the Travers River 1$^1/_2$ hours from the hut. Cross the bridge to join the main track. To reach this swingbridge from Coldwater Hut in the western corner of the lakehead, follow the track from behind the hut, which climbs at first but then stays on the flats. The Hukere Stream is bridged and further upstream from this crossing the swingbridge over the Travers is reached, 1$^1/_2$ hours from the lake. Hopeless Creek, flowing in from the west, is reached after 1 hour from the swingbridge and is bridged 3 minutes upstream from the junction. From Hopeless Creek the track follows the river at first but then gradually climbs away to avoid a gorge, rejoining the river not far below John Tait Hut (DOC, 30–35 bunks, wood/coal stove) 2$^1/_2$ hours from Hopeless Creek.

John Tait Hut (820 m) to Upper Travers Hut (1310 m): 3 hours, Grade 2.

The valley continues to narrow above John Tait, and after crossing Cupola Stream the track climbs high above a gorge. Descending back to the river the track then crosses to the true right, and keeping out of rough going in the riverbed emerges on a tussock-covered flat in the head of the valley. The Upper Travers Hut (DOC, 16 bunks, wood stove) surveys this flat over which looms the magnificent east face of Mt Travers.

Upper Travers Hut (1310 m) to West Sabine (660 m) via Travers Saddle (1800 m): 6–9 hours, Grade 2–3.

Travers Saddle is one of the most popular crossings in the park and in good summer conditions is suitable for most fit trampers. It should not be attempted in bad or winter conditions without suitable experience and equipment. The two obvious passes at the head of the valley are often mistaken for Travers

Saddle. It is in fact further to the west and not visible from the hut. To reach the saddle, cross the stream to the west of the hut and follow the poles up the valley floor before turning west and climbing steeply up an old scree slope. At the top of this slope the gradient eases and the poled route winds in a southwesterly direction up to Travers Saddle. From here follow the poles which drop down and around to the right through the bushline to reach an open gully. Descend into the gully and pick up a track at the bottom which continues down to the East Branch of the Sabine River. After 15 minutes on the valley floor, the track crosses to the true left bank on a bridge over a spectacular cleft gorge, and begins the descent to West Sabine Hut (DOC, 36 bunks, wood stove) a few minutes up the West Branch of the Sabine on the true right. For routes in the Sabine Valley see page 77.

Travers Valley (670 m) to Lake Angelus Hut (1650 m) via Hukere Stream: 4–6 hours, Grade 2–3.

The valley down which the Hukere Stream tumbles is dramatically beautiful, with quiet clearings in its head and ringed by a bluffed head wall and mountains on either side. Lake Angelus itself is a large and pretty alpine tarn. From the junction of Hukere Stream and the Travers River (1 hour from the lake) follow the track up the true right of the stream. After 2–3 hours of rough travel the track levels out before beginning a sharp climb up the head wall of the valley. Above the bush a sporadically poled route leads steeply upwards, threading out to the right of the main bluff to emerge a few minutes north of Lake Angelus Hut (DOC, 35–40 bunks, wood/coal stove — own cooker essential) on the route to Robert Ridge (see p. 76). When snow-covered the top of this route is avalanche prone and requires alpine experience and equipment.

Travers Valley (730 m) to Hopeless Creek Hut (1040 m) via Hopeless Creek: 2¹/₂ hours, Grade 2.

Below the steep bluffs in its head the Hopeless Valley is a gentle and pretty tributary of the Travers. The track leaves from the bridge over Hopeless Creek on the true right bank. Midway up the valley it crosses and re-crosses the main creek, eventually reaching Hopeless Creek Hut (DOC, 12 bunks, wood stove) nestled on the valley floor. For the route to Lake Angelus see p. 77.

Travers Valley (820 m) to Cupola Hut (1400 m): 2¹/₂ hours, Grade 2.

Cupola Creek and basin separate two of the park's highest peaks, Mt Hopeless and Mt Cupola. The track up the valley leaves the Travers Valley track above John Tait Hut. After crossing a bridge over Cupola Creek height is steadily gained until the main creek forks. Follow the track up the more southerly fork until it heads off on a steep ascent to Cupola Hut (DOC, 8 bunks, wood stove) perched just below the bushline. There is a dramatic view of the south face of Mt Hopeless from the front window.

Mt Robert carpark (880 m) to Lake Angelus Hut (1650 m) via Robert Ridge: 5–7 hours, Grade 2–4.

The route along Robert Ridge to Lake Angelus is, in fine summer conditions, a straightforward alpine tramp with magnificent and varied views. It is very exposed to the weather, however, and should not be attempted without good conditions and adequate equipment. The Pinchgut Track (see p. 71) gives the easiest access to the shelter above the Mt Robert skifield in the second basin on Robert Ridge. From the shelter follow along the ridge top above the second and third basins until near the end of the third basin. Here, sidle across the scree slope to the saddle below the outcrop known as Rocky Julius. Drop off around the base of the bluffs on the western side of the ridge and edge around this west-facing basin before regaining the ridge overlooking the fourth basin which drops towards the Travers Valley. Apart from some minor deviations, the route sticks to the ridge until it peters out at the base of a short climb to the rim of the fifth basin in which Lake Angelus lies. Metal poles mark the route from here down to Lake Angelus Hut (DOC, 36 bunks, wood/coal stove – own cooker essential) on the shores of the lake. For routes on from Mt Angelus see below.

Lake Angelus Hut (1650 m) to Hopeless Creek Hut (1040 m) via Sunset Saddle (1890 m): 4–5 hours, Grade 4.

This is a fine weather alpine crossing with good views, and features a number of picturesque tarns en route. Hopeless Creek is heavily bluffed in its head and good visibility is essential for this route. The Hopeless Creek side of the route is also avalanche-prone in winter. From the Angelus Hut follow around the lake and head off southwest to the far end of Hinapouri Tarn. Sunset Saddle is the low point immediately to the west of Mt Angelus, reached by climbing on a southerly bearing. On the other side of the saddle initially keep to the left to avoid a small bluff. Gain a small ridge between the two larger tarns and follow this down to the lower tarn. After crossing this tarn's outlet, sidle down to the right to avoid very steep bluffs directly below the tarn. Wind down through steep tussock and scree between the bluffs to a large scree slope on the southern side of the valley which gives access to the valley floor. At the bush edge on the true right of the creek a marked track leads to Hopeless Creek Hut (DOC, 12 bunks, wood stove). For a track to the Travers Valley see page 74.

Mt Robert carpark (880 m) to Speargrass Hut (1070 m): 2¹/₂ hours, Grade 2.

On the western boundary of the park the Speargrass Valley follows along under Robert Ridge. The track begins from the Mt Robert carpark, descending gradually to Speargrass Creek. Following the creek it works its way to the valley head where Speargrass Hut (DOC, 6 bunks, wood stove) sits amid a clearing of large tussocks. There is a marked route up Speargrass Creek to the ridge above Lake Angelus.

Speargrass Hut (1070 m) to Sabine Hut, Lake Rotoroa (460 m): 5 hours, Grade 2–3.

This track completes an all-weather link from St Arnaud with the tracks at the head of Lake Rotoroa. From the hut it climbs for 15 minutes to a forested saddle, maintains a gentle gradient until reaching the Howard Saddle where it descends to Lake Rotoroa and the Sabine Hut (DOC, 16 bunks, wood stove). For routes from Sabine Hut see below.

OTHER ROUTES AROUND THE TRAVERS VALLEY
The Arnst River
The only major stream draining the St Arnaud Range, the Arnst River is untracked. The best route to gain the wide basin at its head is on the true right, keeping high to avoid gorges in the lower half of the river. In good conditions there is an unmarked but straightforward route north along the crest of the St Arnaud Range past the Rainbow Skifield to the St Arnaud Ridge Track (see p. 71).

Above the head of Lake Rotoroa
Two major rivers, the Sabine and the D'Urville, flow into the head of Lake Rotoroa. Their long, bushclad valleys and the alpine crossings out of these catchments offer fine tramping.

Rotoroa (460 m) to Sabine Hut (460 m): 6–7 hours, Grade 2.

A reasonable track stretches for 18 km up the eastern side of Lake Rotoroa. It begins at the northern end of the picnic ground at Lake Rotoroa and follows the lake shore all the way to the Sabine Hut (DOC, 16 bunks, woodstove) at the head of the lake.

Sabine Hut (460 m) to Lake Angelus Hut (1650 m) via Mt Cedric (1770 m): 4–6 hours, Grade 2–3.

This route connects the Sabine Valley with the Travers Valley and Lake Rotoiti via Lake Angelus. An alpine crossing, it is exposed to the weather and requires some experience. From behind the hut follow a marked and uncompromising track straight up to the bushline. Here a poled route rises up onto Mt Cedric and follows the ridge in a dogleg to gain the rim of the Angelus basin. A cairned and poled route drops off the ridge on a northeast bearing to the lake and the Lake Angelus Hut (DOC, 36 bunks, wood/coal stove — own cooker essential) on the far side. Water should be carried as there is none along the route. For routes from Lake Angelus see pages 75-76.

Sabine Hut to West Sabine (660 m): 5 hours, Grade 2.

Below the forks the Sabine Valley mostly gives easy tramping through beech forest and the occasional clearing. From the hut follow the well-formed track to where a bridge spans a deep and gorged section of the river. On the far bank the track climbs through a small saddle before rejoining the river, staying on the true left all the way to the West Sabine Hut (DOC, 36 bunks, wood stove) which is across the bridge and a few minutes up on the true right bank of the West Sabine River.

West Sabine (660 m) to Blue Lake Hut (1190 m): 3–4 hours, Grade 2.

Blue Lake, tucked high in the head of the West Sabine Valley and renowned for its extraordinarily vivid colouring, is an enchanting place to visit. The track to Blue Lake winds up the true left bank of the West Sabine from the forks, passing through forest and clearings to reach an obvious basin. Here the track veers left and climbs steadily up a forested hillside to reach Blue Lake Hut (DOC, 16 bunks, wood stove), set back from the lake. For a good view down on the lake, and of the much larger Lake Constance above, climb up the hill at the southern end of the lake — there is a marked track through the trees.

Blue Lake Hut (1190 m) to Waiau Valley Head (1370 m) via Waiau Pass (1830 m): 6–8 hours, Grade 3–4.

Waiau Pass above the head of Lake Constance is a high, exposed crossing requiring good summer conditions. If snow-covered it requires alpine equipment and experience. It gives access to the Waiau Valley and from there the D'Urville (see p. 79) and Matakitaki Valleys (see p. 81), as well as the St James Walkway. At the southern end of Blue Lake a route through the trees leads up to Lake Constance. Both shorelines of the lake are usually impassable. To reach its head take a lightly cairned route leading from the lower end of the lake high above the bluffs on the western shore, dropping back down an obvious gully to the lake. From here follow the lake shore to the flats at the lake head. Up the valley above these flats, a sign marks the beginning of the route up a large shingle slide on the eastern side of the alley which climbs to pick up metal poles on a shelf near the top of this slide. These lead around to the south and up to Waiau Pass on the park boundary. From the pass, poles and cairns wind down away to the right (west) into the head of the valley. When travelling in the opposite direction it is essential to pick up cairns in the valley floor marking the beginning of this route. If you intend walking down the Waiau Valley to reach the St James Walkway (1 long day) you will require the permission of Mr Jim Stevenson, St James Station, Hanmer Springs, ph (03) 315 7066.

Blue Lake Hut (1190 m) to Ella Hut (670 m), D'Urville Valley via Moss Pass (1770 m): 5–8 hours, Grade 3–4.

Moss Pass is a popular crossing, less strenuous when approached from Blue Lake. It is an exposed alpine route requiring good summer conditions. Snow often persists well into the spring, and alpine experience and equipment are essential when it is snow-covered. From Blue Lake Hut follow poles west up to the base of a small stream, keeping alongside the stream until a scree slope is reached. Climb westward to an obvious north-facing shoulder where Moss Pass is visible as the northernmost notch on the skyline. Traverse the scree to the base of a steep gully, often snow-filled and up which poles lead to the pass. On the D'Urville side the poles should be carefully followed to avoid bluffs, initially on a southerly line and then on a westerly bearing to the bushline. Here a marked track drops steeply to the valley floor. Cross the bridge over the D'Urville River to pick up the track on the true left leading downstream to the Ella Hut (DOC, 16 bunks, wood stove). See below for routes in D'Urville Valley.

D'Urville Hut (460 m) to Ella Hut (670 m) via Morgans Hut (550 m) and D'Urville Valley: 8 hours, Grade 2.

Though deceptively long and heavily bushed, the D'Urville Valley generally gives easy walking. From D'Urville Hut on the lake edge follow the track on the true left bank through grassy flats and forest for about 4 hours to Morgans Hut (DOC, 14 bunks, wood stove). Continue on the true left for a further 4 hours of easy going to reach Ella Hut (DOC, 16 bunks, wood stove).

Ella Hut (670 m) to head of East Matakitaki (1310 m) via D'Urville Bivvy (1010 m) and David Saddle (1800 m): 7–10 hours, Grade 2–4.

In good summer conditions this is a straightforward crossing in a remote and beautiful area of the park. From Ella Hut continue on the track on the true left of the river, reaching the D'Urville Bivvy (DOC, 2 bunks, wood stove) in about 4 hours. Twenty minutes above the bivvy the marked track fades out where a stream on the right joins the main river. Climb up the true right of this stream into a snowgrass basin where the route to David Saddle, the low point to the southeast, is straightforward. From the saddle the easiest descent is down an obvious and steep southwest/northeast-running fault line. For routes in the East Matakitaki see page 81.

D'Urville Bivvy (1010 m) to head of East Matakitaki (1400 m) via Upper D'Urville Pass (1828 m): 6–8 hours, Grade 3–4.

This crossing into the East Matakitaki generally takes longer than the David Saddle route (see above) though it has an easier descent than David Saddle. It requires clear conditions. From the D'Urville Bivvy (see above) follow the track on the true left until it fades out where a stream on the right joins the main river. Stay on the true left of the main river until the next tributary coming in from the true left is reached. Climb up this creek into basins above and on to the obvious pass on the true left. From the pass drop to a small tarn and then down a gully to the left of the tarn to the valley floor.

D'Urville Bivvy (1010 m) to Waiau Valley (1370 m) via Thompson Pass (1800 m): 6–7 hours, Grade 2–4.

Thompson Pass provides an easier alternative to Waiau Pass for access into the Waiau Valley, though it is still an alpine crossing requiring clear summer conditions. From the D'Urville Bivvy (see p. 79) follow the track on the true left until it fades out where a stream on the right joins the main river. Stay on the true left of the main river until a large scree is passed on the true right. Here, cross the river and climb on a diagonal line up through the tussock to a steep scree running down through rocky outcrops. Continue up to Thompson Pass, the lowest point on the ridge line. (Note that on map NZMS 1 S40, 1982 edition, Thompson Pass is incorrectly marked.) From Thompson Pass an obvious fault-line gut leads down to Lake Thompson. To reach the floor of the Waiau Valley it is easier to travel on the western side of the stream draining the lake. If you intend walking down the Waiau Valley to the St James Walkway (1 long day) you will require the permission of Mr Jim Stevenson, St James Station, Hanmer Springs, ph (03) 315 7066.

D'Urville Hut (460 m) to Sabine Hut (460 m): 2–3 hours, Grade 2.

The track which connects these two huts and valleys at the head of Lake Rotoroa leaves the D'Urville Valley Track about 10 minutes from the D'Urville Hut. After crossing the river it skirts under the base of Mt Misery to the bridge over the Sabine River, about 45 minutes from the Sabine Hut (DOC, 16 bunks, wood stove) on the lake shore.

D'Urville Hut (460 m) to Mt Misery Bivvy (1560 m): 3–4 hours, Grade 2.

Mt Misery separates the D'Urville and Sabine Valleys and provides commanding views down the lake and of the surrounding mountains. It is climbed on a track which branches off the track between the D'Urville and Sabine Valleys (see above) close to the true right bank of the D'Urville River, and leads steeply up through the forest to the bushline on the end of the Mahanga Range. The cosy Mt Misery Bivvy (DOC, 3 bunks, no heating or cooking facilities) sits by a tarn under the Mt Misery trig.

OTHER ROUTES ABOVE THE HEAD OF LAKE ROTOROA

East Sabine

Beyond where the track ascends to the Travers Saddle (see p. 74) the attractive East Sabine Valley is untracked. Reasonable travel on the true left leads to open country and a large unnamed tarn in the head of the valley.

Tiraumea Valley

The marked Tiraumea Track leaves from the lower D'Urville Valley 30 minutes up from the lake shore, and leads westward out of the park. Zigzagging up to the Tiraumea Saddle the track then leads down the valley to Tiraumea Hut and eventually the Tutaki Road.

Mole Saddle

Further up the valley another route (no longer being maintained) out of the D'Urville Valley and the park leads up Bull Creek, 1 hour from the D'Urville Hut. On the true right a track follows up Bull Creek and then out to Mole Saddle. From here the route drops down to the Mole Shelter, Mole Stream and then out to the Tutaki Road.

THE MATAKITAKI AND GLENROY AREA

The tracks in these two remote, beautiful and bushclad valleys are not as frequently walked as those in other parts of the park, though the tracks are all marked and in good condition.

Matakitaki Road end (400 m) to Downies Hut (550 m), Matakitaki Valley: 4–5 hours, Grade 1.

The section of the Matakitaki Valley below Downies Hut is Crown leasehold land, and the river flats are grazed. Just before the end of the Tutaki Road a rough road turns off to the left and leads to a locked gate. From here follow the four-wheel-drive track up the true right of the Matakitaki River through forest and across broad river flats to Downies Hut (private, though available for public use, 4 bunks, open fire) at the southern end of a large flat. Permission is required from the Mt Ella Station Manager, ph (03) 523 9414.

Downies Hut (550 m) to East Matakitaki Hut (910 m): 5–6 hours, Grade 2.

From Downies Hut pick up the track on the true right of the river which enters the park about 2 km past the hut. Above the Burn Creek junction the track leaves the river to avoid a gorge, reaching the forks of the east and west branches after 3–4 hours' walking. A three-wire walkwire spans the east branch above the forks and a track on the true left gives reasonable travelling to the East Matakitaki Hut (DOC, 4 bunks, open fire) in a clearing by the river. Above this hut there is no marked track but easy travelling on the true left gives access to the attractive head of this valley and the two passes that lead out (see pp. 79-80) into the D'Urville. There is also the option of a high walk in good conditions around the head of the D'Urville Valley to gain Thompson Pass (see p. 80). As well, 30 minutes above the hut, a marked track climbs from the true left of the valley floor up to the Una Basin, about a 2-hour climb.

Downies Hut (550 m) to Bob's Hut (820 m) via west branch of Matakitaki River: 6 hours, Grade 2.

See above for route to forks. If required, walkwires span both the west and east branches above the forks. The track up the west branch can be picked up on the true left, and takes about 1¹/₂ hours to reach the clearing where Bob's Hut (DOC, 4 bunks, open fire) is sited. Above Bob's Hut a marked track up the true right of the west branch gives access to a pass into the Glenroy Valley (see below). As well, there is a straightforward route from the southern side of the basin at the head of the west branch over into the headwaters of the Maruia River and Ada Hut on the St James Walkway.

Downies Hut (550 m) to Burn Creek Bivvy (1250 m): 5–6 hours, Grade 3.

From the track on the true right of the Matakitaki River cross the river to pick up a rough route, initially on the true right of the creek, which leads to the bushline and the small Burn Creek Bivvy (DOC, 2 bunks, open fire).

OTHER ROUTES IN THE MATAKITAKI VALLEY

McKellar Stream

Dropping down from under Mt Ella, a marked route follows McKellar Stream up from the valley floor.

Downie Creek

From Downies Hut a marked route (no longer being maintained) leads up on the true right side of the valley to the Mt Dorothy Basin, an impressive cirque on the Ella Range.

Nardoo Creek

After crossing the Matakitaki River a route follows up the Nardoo Creek to the bushline. From here it is possible to drop into Junction Creek, or to traverse the Emily Peaks to the head of Burn Creek (see above).

THE GLENROY VALLEY

Glenroy Valley Road end (430 m) to Upper Glenroy Hut (790 m): 11 hours, Grade 2.

From the road end in the Glenroy Valley the track crisscrosses the river for the first 6 hours to the Mid-Glenroy Hut (DOC, 4 bunks, open fire). The walking is generally on wide river flats. The track is not in the park until well above the Mid-Glenroy Hut, reaching the dilapidated Upper Glenroy Hut (DOC, 3 bunks, open fire) after about 4–5 hours. An eastern fork of the Glenroy gives access to straightforward passes into the Matakitaki and Maruia catchments. The tracks in the Glenroy are no longer being maintained.

paparoa *national park*

The natural attractions of the South Island's west coast are so widely lauded that it is remarkable that the western lowlands of the Paparoa Range have only come to the public's broader attention within the last 15 years. This area, sandwiched between the jumbled crest of the Paparoa Range and the battered coastline between Greymouth and Westport, is of great natural significance. Features include a dramatic, rocky coastline; a large basin of spectacular limestone formations and lowland forest; and peaks and ridges of the range itself.

The Paparoas were thrust into the limelight during the 1970s when proposals to log the tall forest of the western lowlands prompted a vigorous conservation campaign. The area's biological significance was quickly and unquestionably established, and along with its obvious scenic and recreational values gave great weight to pleas for the creation of a national park. These were ultimately successful, with the gazetting of the Paparoa National Park in 1987, encompassing the heart of the western lowlands.

The core of the park is a large depression in the land between the sea and the mountains, formed from a huge area of warped limestone framed by high scarps. Over many millions of years the buckling of the earth and erosion by water of the soft limestone has left an extraordinary landscape. The rivers flowing west from the mountains have carved deep canyons through the scarps, the walls sometimes towering hundreds of metres above the riverbed. Between the rivers lie chaotic stretches of karst country — limestone with enormous sinkholes, cliffs, overhangs, blind valleys and disappearing streams, while the whole area is underlaid by an elaborate system of caves.

On the coast, endless westerly swells pounding the limestone have left a beautiful stretch of cliffs, headlands, beaches and spectacular rock formations. The highway between Greymouth and Westport winds along this coastline and it is this part of the Paparoas that has become best known, especially Punakaiki where the famous pancake rocks and blowholes at Dolomite Point have long been a West Coast tourist attraction.

The karst landscape of the western lowlands is covered in dense forest. The mild climate, heavy rainfall and fertile soils have encouraged a lush inland

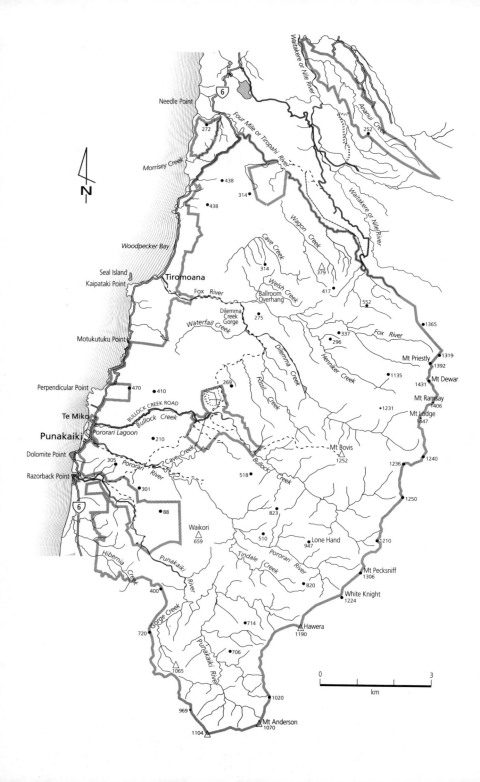

forest of podocarps, beech and broadleaf trees, while the coastal forest is characterised by the wonderful groves of nikau palms, almost tropical in appearance. The size of this lowland forest, and its largely virgin state, make it an extremely important wildlife habitat. In fact it supports the highest concentrations of native forest birds ever recorded in New Zealand.

East of the western lowlands the Paparoa Range rises. The section lying inside the park is composed mainly of granite and gneisses, and is totally different in character from the limestone country below. Here the rocks are very old, and have been shaped into a chain of relatively low but very rugged mountains. This craggy range presents a real challenge for the tramper, with thick beech forest cloaking its flanks, impenetrable subalpine scrub in places and persistently bad weather.

There was a small, hardy population of Maori living on the coast when the first Europeans arrived. They had been established there for many hundreds of years, most likely encouraged by the presence of pounamu (jade or greenstone) on the West Coast.

The early European navigators, Abel Tasman, Captain James Cook, and later Dumont D'Urville, observed the wild coastline and jagged peaks of the Paparoas from the sea. None of them landed — the first to set foot were probably sealers. In 1846 the first exploration of the area occurred when Charles Heaphy and Thomas Brunner, guided by the Maori Ekehu, struggled down the Paparoa coastline. Brunner returned the following year on a courageous 18-month journey from Nelson that took him as far south as Paringa. A gold strike in 1864 marked a turning point on the isolated West Coast, with thousands of miners flooding into the region over the next few years. Strikes at the southern end of the Paparoa Range, and at Brighton and Charleston, north of Punakaiki, began to open up the area. In about 1867 the Razorback Road (now the Inland Pack Track) was cut through the western lowlands to avoid the treacherous route up the coast. It was used until early last century, when a coastal track was finally built.

The Paparoa National Park offers tramping conditions quite unlike those found in any other New Zealand national park. Although the scope for lengthy trips on established tracks and routes is limited, the trips currently available are superb. There is mostly easy walking on very accessible tracks, and as long as trampers are wary of flooded rivers and don't wander off into the broken karst country the area is quite safe.

Information

PAPAROA NATIONAL PARK VISITOR CENTRE

The Paparoa National Park Visitor Centre is at Punakaiki, and has comprehensive displays and information on the walking tracks. The visitor centre is open seven days a week from 9.00 a.m. until 4.30 p.m., and stays open until 6.00 p.m. during the summer holidays. The address for enquiries is:

Paparoa National Park Visitor Centre
Department of Conservation
Post Box 1
Punakaiki
Phone (03) 731 1895
Fax (03) 731 1896

ACCESS

All the walks are reached from SH 6 between Westport and Greymouth. The only other road into the park is the scenic access road to the state-owned farm in Bullock Creek, which branches off SH 6 just north of Punakaiki — please leave all gates as you found them; cars, dogs and guns are not allowed on the farm, and be aware that this road is subject to flooding after rain.

TRANSPORT SERVICES

Intercity buses operate through Punakaiki, between Westport and Greymouth. Kea Tours (phone 0800 532 868) offer transport between Greymouth and Punakaiki, as well as tours to other places on the Coast, on demand. Both Greymouth and Westport are serviced by bus, with a railcar link between Greymouth and Christchurch. There are airports at Westport and Hokitika.

ACCOMMODATION

Camping grounds: The Buller District Council operates a motor camp at Punakaiki, with all facilities, including cabins and bunkrooms. There are also camping grounds outside the park, at Greymouth, Charleston, Carter's Beach (south of Westport) and in Westport itself.

Hostels, motels and hotels: Both Westport and Greymouth have numerous backpacker hostels, motels and hotels. There are motels and two backpacker lodges at Punakaiki.

SERVICES

At Punakaiki there is a store and cafe while Westport and Greymouth are fully serviced towns.

WEATHER

The low altitude, the influence of the warm Westland oceanic current, and the prevailing moist westerly winds ensure that the western lowlands enjoy a mild and wet climate but surprisingly high sunshine hours. The most settled times of the year are from January to April, as well as mid-winter, when the West Coast often enjoys clear weather. The climate of the Paparoa Range itself is different from down on the coast, with a higher rainfall and frequent cloud.

MAPS

Parkmap 273/12 of Paparoa National Park covers the entire park, and has tracks marked. The Topomap 260 series K30 Punakaiki is also useful but does not cover the entire park.

FURTHER READING

Paparoa National Park (Department of Conservation, Hokitika, 1987) is an illustrated booklet which provides a good introduction to the park, while Terry Summer's *Buller Walks* (Nikau Press, 1987) is a useful and condensed guide to most of the walks within the park.

Short walks

Fox River Caves: 3 hours return, Grade 2–3.
The walk up the Fox River to the caves, and an exploration of the upper cave, is a marvellous and safe way of seeing something of the cave systems that riddle the limestone country of the Paparoas. A torch is essential if entering a cave. Begin at SH 6 just north of the Fox River Bridge where a short gravel road leads down to the beginning of the track. The track follows up the true right bank of the river, in most places on an old miners' pack-track, to reach a junction where the Inland Pack Track crosses to the true left bank. Here the benched track to the caves continues up the true right, eventually turning and climbing steeply up to the entrance. The upper 'tourist' cave is safe for those with torches, but do not enter the lower cave as it can be hazardous. The passage in the upper cave has some pretty formations which must not be damaged.

Fox River Track to Ballroom Overhang: 3–5 hours return, Grade 2–3.
The canyon of the Fox River has many attractions apart from the caves (above). Towering limestone cliffs, thick forest, an attractive river and the famous 'Ballroom Overhang' warrant a walk up this river. The Fox River Track as far as Dilemma Creek is actually the beginning of the Inland Pack Track

(see p. 89). Begin as for the Fox River Caves, but at the marked ford cross the Fox River to pick up the track on the true left. This ford is normally straightforward, though it should not be attempted if the river is in flood. The track continues up the true left to the entrance of Dilemma Creek and another ford where the route to the Ballroom Overhang is signposted, about 1$^1/_2$ hours from the road. (When the river is low this point can easily be reached by scrambling up the riverbed from the first ford; this alternative route offers far more spectacular views than the track through the forest.) Past the second ford, continue on up the bed of the Fox for 30 minutes, crossing and recrossing to reach the Ballroom Overhang, a massive overhang alongside the river. The overhang is renowned as a sheltered campsite, with a grassy floor, and a toilet provided. On the return trip the more adventurous can detour up into the delightful mosses, ferns and forest of Welsh Creek, which flows in from the true right of the Fox below the Ballroom Overhang.

Truman Track: 30 minutes return, Grade 1–3.
About 3 km north of the visitor centre at Punakaiki, a carpark on SH 6 marks the beginning of the Truman Track. This lovely walk leads down to the dramatic Te Miko coastline, initially through coastal forest and then through scrub and flax. From the clifftop a track leads down to the first beach and here, at low tide, it is possible to explore the fascinating area of cliffs, caves and rock pools to the north. Great caution is necessary, though; be watchful of incoming tides and slippery rocks.

Punakaiki Cavern: 10 minutes return, Grade 2.
At the base of the high limestone cliffs that loom above the road just north of the visitor centre there is a small cave that can be easily and safely explored. It is best to park at the visitor centre and walk down the road to the beginning of the track. Steps and a short track lead to the base of the cliff and the beginning of the passage, which extends 138 m into the hill. A torch is necessary.

Dolomite Point Walk: 20–30 minute round trip, Grade 1.
The remarkable concentration of sculptured limestone at Dolomite Point has long been one of the West Coast's best known tourist attractions, famous for its blowholes and the Pancake Rocks. Dolomite Point is worth visiting in all conditions. On clear, still days the Pancake Rocks are fascinating to visit, and the views north (to Perpendicular Point) and south (sometimes as far as Mt Cook) are magnificent. At high tide when a big sea is running the atmosphere of this place is very different. The sight and sound of water being forced into the holes and cracks and erupting out in explosions of spray and foam is unforgettable. The track (suitable for wheelchairs if assistance is provided) begins opposite the visitor centre and leads down through forest and scrub to

a junction where the track divides to loop around the blowholes and the Pancake Rocks. It is dangerous to stray off the tracks.

Pororari River Track: 30 minutes to 3 hours return, Grade 1–2.
The track up the Pororari River offers access to the extraordinarily beautiful gorges and forest that grace this river. It begins 1¹/₂ km north of the visitor centre and leads into a grove of nikau palms, emerging 15 minutes later at Punjabi Beach, a good turn-around point for those with limited time. The track continues up the forested gorge to flatter country, meeting the Inland Pack Track after about an hour and a quarter. Those wishing to carry on can cross over into the Punakaiki River (see below).

Pororari Punakaiki Loop: 3 hours round trip, Grade 2.
The trip up the lower Pororari gorge to meet the Inland Pack Track, then over a low saddle and down the Punakaiki River to the highway, offers a good look at the limestone landforms and lush forest that characterise this area. Follow the Pororari River Track (see above) from its starting point for an hour and fifteen minutes to reach the Inland Pack Track. Here turn right and follow the Pack Track over the limestone ridge that separates the two rivers, with good views out to the Paparoa Range en route. The track drops steeply from the saddle and then eases off to reach a rough road and a normally easy ford over the Punakaiki River. It is a 2 km walk from the beginning of this road down to the State Highway then along to the visitor centre.

Tramping

Within the Paparoa National Park there is currently only one established tramping route, the Inland Pack Track, though there is a marked route from Bullock Creek up to the summit of Mt Bovis — consult DOC staff for further information on this trip.

THE INLAND PACK TRACK
The Inland Pack Track runs in a loop through the extraordinary limestone country of the western Paparoas, and provides a unique tramping trip. With towering limestone canyons, outstanding lowland forest and the backdrop of the Paparoa Range, this trip should not be overlooked. The track was formed in 1867 to avoid the wild coastline between the Fox River and Punakaiki, and was known as the Razorback Road. Generally it is an easy walk, especially where it follows the old pack-track, though in many places it is only a riverbed route, which is very susceptible to flooding after rain. There are no huts, so a tent must be carried. It is usually a two-day trip, though it could be done in

one long day, or in three days by someone wanting to explore the area thoroughly. It can be walked from either end.

Fox River Bridge (10 m) to Fossil Creek (50 m): 2 hours, Grade 2–3.

The beginning of the Inland Pack Track up the Fox River as far as Dilemma Creek is described on page 87. Dilemma Creek flows in from the true left bank of the Fox, an obvious junction of the two rivers' canyons. If following the track, do not drop off into the Fox but continue until Dilemma Creek is reached. From here the route is along the riverbed of this particularly beautiful canyon, with many crossings of the normally gentle creek. After about an hour and a quarter the canyon opens out and Fossil Creek is reached flowing in from the true left bank. Here the river flats provide a fine campsite.

Fossil Creek (50 m) to Punakaiki (10 m): 6–7 hours, Grade 1–2.

Follow up the delightful bed of Fossil Creek for about 30 minutes. Here, markers on the true right indicate the beginning of the track, which heads off to the southwest through the beech and podocarp forest. When the track ascends on to a dry ridge there are good views back to the impressive bluff that separates Dilemma Creek from the Fox River, and to the distant peaks of the range beyond. Dropping off the ridge, the track eventually emerges from the forest on to the fringes of the cleared land at Bullock Creek where the track is signposted through to a ford over Bullock Creek. From here follow the road south to a marked junction where the Bullock Creek Road heads west to the sea. Keep to the farm track which heads southwest from this junction and follow it to the top of a small rise. The Inland Pack Track then leads off into the beech forest. This section meanders gently across the undulating karst landscape (do not stray off the track as there are many dangerous sinkholes) and through the lowland forest to a picturesque ford of the Pororari River, about 2 hours from Bullock Creek. Cross the river to reach a junction where the Pororari River Track (see p. 89) branches off, an alternative route back to Punakaiki. The Inland Pack Track continues south from here, climbing gently to a low saddle, where a lookout 50 m up the ridge to the south gives good views out over the surrounding country. A benched track drops down from the saddle to reach a ford over the Punakaiki River in about 30–40 minutes. From here it is 1 km down the road to the highway, and just over 1 km further north to the Punakaiki Visitor Centre.

arthur's pass *national park*

Arthur's Pass National Park straddles a section of the South Island's mountain divide, and with a foot in both Westland and Canterbury it is a park of impressive contrasts. On the eastern side of the Southern Alps sprawling riverbeds and open beech forests rise up to high mountains. In the west these mountains drop into the wet bush of Westland, where dense tall trees crowd over rough and wild rivers. For those who tramp in the backcountry, or who travel on the highway that cuts through the middle of the park, the experience of this dramatic transition from east to west is the real essence of this national park.

Arthur's Pass is principally an alpine area, dominated always by the rugged peaks of the Southern Alps. Like much of the alps, these mountains are built mostly of greywacke, a crumbly, soft sedimentary rock pushed up into ranges many millions of years ago. Since that time the ongoing cycle of erosion has never ceased. Small glaciers are still to be found (in fact the northernmost in the South Island), but once they were colossal tongues of ice stretching to the coast in the west and as far as the Canterbury Plains in the east. Shaping the mountains and valleys, these glaciers were a major influence on the landscape we see today, though much has changed since they retreated. Weathering and water have carried vast amounts of the crumbling rock down into the valleys — the gravel bed of the Waimakariri River is estimated to be about 300 m thick around the Bealey settlement.

The Southern Alps create a powerful barrier to the prevailing westerly weather systems that roll in off the Tasman Sea. As a consequence, the heaviest rain falls on the western side of the divide, an annual average at Otira of 5000 mm. Compare this with the annual average of 1500 mm at Bealey on the eastern side of the park, and the startling difference in vegetation between the eastern and western sides of the Main Divide is explained.

At lower altitudes on the Westland side, high rainfall and temperate conditions have encouraged lush forests of tall podocarp trees, while higher up, forests of kamahi, totara and brightly flowering rata thrive. Crossing the Alps there is a rapid change in the forest as it quickly becomes a uniform cover

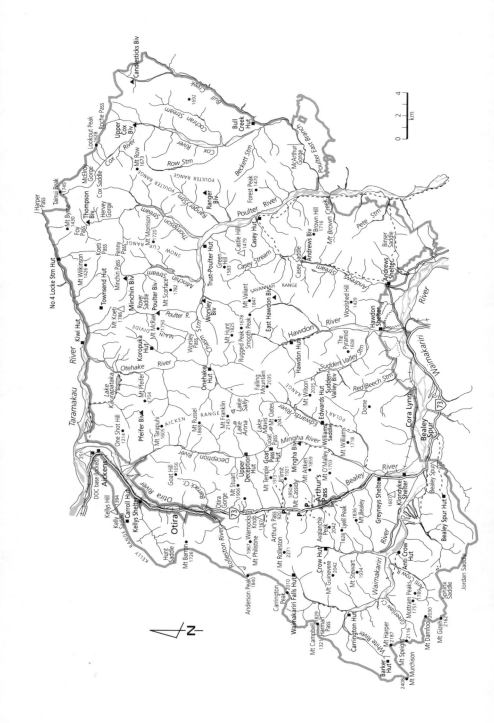

of beech trees, principally the small-leaved mountain beech species. The forest on the east is far drier and more open in structure than that in the west. This rapid transition of forest composition has a marked effect on the wildlife that inhabits these areas — there are notably more bird species in the west than in the east.

It seems that the Arthur's Pass area was never permanently settled by Maori. It saw many visits, however, by parties on hunting expeditions, making social trips to the West Coast or travelling to the Taramakau and the Arahura, the greenstone-bearing rivers of Westland. What is now Harpers Pass on the northern boundary of the park was the most frequently crossed, but Arthur's Pass provided a route as well.

Europeans in search of country on which to graze their sheep were the first to explore the park's eastern and southern boundaries, and the many thousands flocking to the 1860s gold rushes on the West Coast used Harpers Pass and the Taramakau Valley to the north. Instructions to find a more direct route between Canterbury and Westland prompted a young surveyor, Arthur Dudley Dobson, to push a route up the Bealey River and cross the pass at the valley's head. Though it traversed extremely rough and difficult country it became obvious to the provincial government of the day that it provided the best route. So in 1865 road construction was begun, and Arthur Dobson's discovery became known as Arthur's Pass. The completion of the road in 1866 was an impressive engineering feat and saw the beginning of a colourful saga of travel and transport over this pass. Initially it was mostly by horse-drawn coach and dray, but with the massive undertaking of the Otira Tunnel completed in 1923 and the opening of the Midland Railway Line, trains replaced horses. As the road through the spectacular Otira Gorge was gradually improved, motor vehicles joined rail transport to become heavy users of the pass.

The steady flow of travellers passing through this beautiful area since last century ensured that its natural values became well known. New Zealand's eminent early ecologist Dr Leonard Cockayne worked in the area and had a cottage at Kelly's Creek near Otira. It was the enthusiasm of Cockayne and others for preserving this wilderness that prompted the Government to set aside two large reserves in the Otira and Waimakariri Valleys in 1901. Interest continued to grow in the area, with the result that Arthur's Pass National Park was officially born in 1929.

Arthur's Pass offers a fine selection of tramping, but is possibly best known for the trips that link valleys on both sides of the Alps with Main Divide crossings. In good summer conditions a number of these crossings are within reach of average trampers. Others present more challenges for experienced parties, especially during winter. All passes in the park are subjected to the full brunt of winter storms and snowfalls and at these times require mountain-eering experience and equipment. For those not interested in 'pass-hopping', the valleys themselves offer fine, often easy and relaxed trips, with a choice between the open beech forest and braided riverbeds of the east, and the more heavily forested and enclosed valleys of the west. Arthur's Pass is a true tramper's park: varied, accessible and beautiful.

Information

PARK VISITOR CENTRE AND AREA OFFICE

The park visitor centre and area office is in the Arthur's Pass township and offers the usual information, services and display. The office is open from 8.00 a.m. until 5.00 p.m. seven days a week. The address for enquiries is:

> Arthur's Pass Visitor Centre (SH 73)
> PO Box 8
> Arthur's Pass
> Phone (03) 318 9211
> Fax (03) 318 9120

Intentions are best recorded at the park visitor centre, which must be notified at the completion of a trip. Intentions can also be recorded at the Andrews, Hawdon, Klondyke, Greyneys and Kelly Shelters but these intentions are not checked daily and provide information only.

ACCESS

State Highway 73 cuts right through the middle of Arthur's Pass National Park and provides easy access to many parts of the park. SH 73 leads directly from Christchurch, and on the West Coast turns off SH 6 at Kumara Junction. The Hawdon River and the Andrews Stream are reached from a side-road that turns off SH 73 approximately 27 km east of Arthur's Pass township.

TRANSPORT SERVICES

Tranzrail services Arthur's Pass by a daily train through Arthur's Pass and Otira townships, which will stop on request at some smaller stations in the park (freephone 0800 802 802 for information and bookings). The Coast to Coast Shuttle (freephone 0800 800 847) runs a daily return minibus service through Arthur's Pass, between Christchurch and Greymouth, while Alpine Coach and Courier (phone (03) 762 5081 or 0800 274 888) runs a daily minibus service through Arthur's Pass between Greymouth and Christchurch.

ACCOMMODATION

Shelters: There are public shelters (not for overnight use) at the Hawdon River, Andrews Stream, Klondyke Corner, Greyneys Creek, Arthur's Pass Township and Kelly's Creek.

Camping areas: There are no serviced camping grounds in the park, but there are areas suitable for camping with a shelter, toilets and water available at Klondyke Corner, Hawdon River, Andrews Stream, Kelly's Creek and Arthur's Pass township.

Hostels and lodges: There is a 21-bed youth hostel and a backpackers hostel in Arthur's Pass township, as well as a number of club lodges and an outdoor education centre. Some privately owned cottages are available for rent — ask at the visitor centre.

Motels and hotels: There is a motel and a bed-and-breakfast at Arthur's Pass, a hotel (with motel accommodation) at Bealey, and a licensed hotel at Otira.

SERVICES

Arthur's Pass is well serviced with a general store and tearooms, petrol pump, restaurant, cafe, public telephone, public toilets and railway station. Otira has tearooms and a public bar at the hotel.

WEATHER

As it lies in the exposed Southern Alps, Arthur's Pass National Park takes the full brunt of the prevailing westerly weather systems. Consequently the climate is very wet and often windy. Rainfall at Otira in the west is about 5000 mm a year, with Bealey in the rain shadow of the mountains on the eastern boundary receiving dramatically less rainfall, about 1500 mm a year. The weather is generally most unsettled, often for long periods, in the spring and autumn. During winter, snow regularly falls throughout the park and drifts to great depths on the higher slopes. The most favourable weather for tramping is in January, February and March when temperatures are higher and rainfall less. It is worth remembering that during westerly storms the weather will often be more favourable to the east of the Main Divide.

MAPS

Parkmap 273/01 of Arthur's Pass National Park covers the entire park and has huts and tracks marked. For more detailed information trampers should use the Topomap 260 series, K33 Otira, K34 Wilberforce and L33 Dampier.

FURTHER READING

The fourth edition of the *Arthur's Pass National Park Handbook* (Arthur's Pass National Park, 1986) gives the best insight into the natural and social history and the recreational values of the park. The park authorities have published numerous booklets and pamphlets on a variety of recreational, natural and historical subjects. Of particular interest to trampers will be the Arthur's Pass National Park Routeguide series, which covers most of the extended tramps in the park. This 11-part series of pamphlets is available from park headquarters.

Short walks

Many of the short walks in Arthur's Pass National Park take the walker into alpine areas and may become dangerous or difficult in winter conditions. If you are in any doubt as to what conditions you may encounter, then consult the staff at park headquarters before setting out. The short walks described below are listed in the order in which they leave SH 73, travelling from east to west.

Bealey Spur: 4–5 hours return, Grade 2.
From the top of the road leading up through the Bealey settlement, a well-graded track follows up the Bealey Spur, winding past large tarns and through patches of forest broken by stretches of open tussock. There are sweeping views both up and down the Waimakariri en route, and the Bealey Spur Hut (DOC, 6 bunks, open fire) is reached after 2–3 hours.

Old Coach Road Walk: 20 minutes one way, Grade 1, designed for disabled users.
From behind the picnic shelter at Greyneys Shelter on SH 73 a section of the Old Coach Road can be picked up and followed for 20 minutes through the forest. At its northern end a rope trail provides access for the blind or for those with sight who want to shut their eyes and use their other senses as they move through the forest.

Mt Bealey Track: 6–8 hours return, Grade 2–3.
On the south side of Rough Creek at the southern end of Arthur's Pass township a side-road leads from SH 73 to the start of this track. From the valley it climbs steeply for 1½ hours to the bushline. Above the bushline there is no track, but in clear summer conditions the route up the ridge to Mt Bealey is obvious and presents no problems. Walkers are rewarded with a fine view.

Rough Creek Waterfall: 2 hours return, Grade 3.
This is not a foot-track but a route up the bed of Rough Creek to a waterfall. Begin from SH 73 by the bridge over Rough Creek at the southern end of the

Arthur's Pass township. Follow the creekbed up to the first fork, keeping to the western tributary (flowing in from the true left) to reach the Rough Creek Waterfall.

Avalanche Peak Track: 6–8 hours return, Grade 2–3.

The Avalanche Peak Track provides a steep but direct route to the bushline below Avalanche Peak, and gives access to one of the ridges leading to its summit. It is commonly linked with Scotts Track (see below) as the descent route to create a round trip back to the township. The track begins from behind the chapel at Avalanche Creek in Arthur's Pass township and soon starts an unrelenting climb to the bushline. In clear summer conditions, the poled route up the ridge to Avalanche Peak is straightforward and there are spectacular views from the top. Walkers are warned that in winter the basins north and south of Avalanche Peak should never be traversed, as they are prone to avalanche danger.

Scotts Track to Avalanche Peak: 6–8 hours return, Grade 2–3.

Scotts Track offers an easier alternative than the Avalanche Peak Track for climbing Avalanche Peak, and is linked with this track to make a round trip. It leaves SH 73 5 km above Arthur's Pass township just beyond the Devil's Punchbowl Falls Lookout Track, taking 2 hours to gain the bushline. From here in clear summer conditions the ridge provides a straightforward poled route to the summit of Avalanche Peak. Walkers are warned that in winter the basins north and south of Avalanche Peak should never be traversed, as they are prone to avalanche danger.

Bealey Footbridge: 10 minutes return, Grade 1.

At the northern end of the Arthur's Pass township a short road leaves SH 73 and leads to a carpark. Five minutes' walk from the carpark is the Bealey Footbridge over the Bealey River which gives access to a number of walks.

Devil's Punchbowl Falls Track: 1½ hours return, Grade 2.

After crossing the Bealey Footbridge (see above) the track to the Devil's Punchbowl Falls branches to the right, crosses the Devil's Punchbowl Falls Creek and zigzags up to a signposted junction. A left turn leads to a viewpoint of this dramatic waterfall.

Mt Aicken Track: 3–4 hours return to bushline, Grade 2.

From the Bealey Footbridge (see above) the track to the Devil's Punchbowl Falls is followed up to a signposted junction. Here a stiff climb follows the line of an old waterpipe and passes a collapsed tunnel that once formed part of a hydro-electric generating system built for the construction of the Otira Tunnel. The track climbs above a line of bluffs and leads to the bushline and the tussock slopes under Mt Aicken. Beyond here the scramble up the ridge to Mt Aicken is suitable only for those with some alpine experience.

Con's Track to Mt Cassidy and Mt B'Limit: 8 hours return, Grade 2–4.

Above the bushline the routes to Mt Cassidy and Mt B'Limit require good conditions and some alpine experience. Con's Track begins from the Bealey Footbridge (see p. 97) between the Bridal Veil Track and the Devil's Punchbowl Falls Track. It climbs steeply through the forest and then tussock to reach the broken ridge line that leads to Mt Cassidy and Mt B'Limit.

Bridal Veil Walk: 45 minutes one way, Grade 2.

This walk begins across the Bealey Footbridge (see p. 97) and provides an alternative route for those wanting to walk up SH 73, as the track follows up through the forest across from the highway on the east bank of the Bealey River. It passes the Bridal Veil Falls Lookout, crosses the Bridal Veil Stream and rejoins SH 73 below Jacks Hut.

Coral Track to Rome Ridge: 3 hours return, Grade 2.

The Coral Track is most frequently used by climbers as it gives access to Rome Ridge, one of the popular climbing routes on Mt Rolleston. Provided walkers go no further than the bushline, it provides a safe and direct route to the tops and fine views down into the Bealey Valley. The track begins off SH 73 on the western side of McGrath's Creek, and follows up a steep spur to emerge below Rome Ridge.

Upper Bealey Valley Track: 3–4 hours return, Grade 1–3.

This walk leads into the upper reaches of the Bealey River under the 2271 m peak of Mt Rolleston. The track begins from a carpark 3 km north of the Arthur's Pass township on SH 73, crossing the Bealey Chasm after 10 minutes and cutting through bush before dropping down to the river. The Bealey riverbed is then followed to the end point of this walk, a spectacular gorge where avalanche debris collects off Mt Rolleston. The upper area of the valley is exposed to avalanches in winter and spring and should be avoided at these times.

Dobson Nature Walk: $1/2$–$1^1/2$ hours, Grade 1, pamphlet available.

This nature walk begins off SH 73 just before the top of Arthur's Pass opposite the Dobson Memorial and about 5 km from the Arthur's Pass township. Park cars in the Temple Basin carpark across the road. There are two variations possible: a shorter loop taking about 30 minutes; and the longer track on boardwalks through alpine tussock and bogs to connect with the Upper Otira Valley Track. A right turn at this junction leads out to SH 73.

Temple Basin Track: 3 hours, Grade 1–2.

This walk up the access track to the Temple Basin Skifield provides fine views of the surrounding mountains. It leaves from a carpark below the summit of Arthur's Pass, 5 km from Arthur's Pass township. The first 45 minutes' walking is up a zigzagging four-wheel-drive track to the base of a line of bluffs.

Beyond here the next 45 minutes of walking is on a foot track up to the ski huts and the public George Lockwood Shelter. In good conditions and with some alpine experience the ridge on the left of the ski tow can be climbed to reach a benched track. This sidles around to the Downhill Basin, which can be climbed to Temple Col at its head, with fine views down into the Mingha Valley.

Upper Otira Valley Track: 2–4 hours, Grade 2.

This track winds into the dramatic Upper Otira Valley, beginning from SH 73 just past Lake Misery on the West Coast side of Arthur's Pass. Passing through subalpine scrub and tussock it takes an hour to reach a footbridge over the river. In spring and winter walkers should go no further than here, as there is often avalanche danger in the head of the valley. In summer, however, the track continues up into the upper basin of the Otira until the track fades out at the base of Mt Rolleston.

Warnock's Knob: 5 hours return, Grade 1–4.

For most people this is a summer trip requiring good conditions. It follows the Upper Otira Valley Track (see above) to the footbridge over the Otira River. From here there is no marked route. Follow downstream to a large scree slope and climb up to a depression between Warnock's Knob and the bluffs of Mt Philistine. From here pick a route onto Warnock's Knob where there are particularly good views down into the Otira Gorge.

Barrack Creek and Goat Hill Track: 5–9 hours return, Grade 2–4.

This stiff climb leaves from the eastern side of the Otira Road Bridge off SH 73. The rough track is found a little way up the northern side (true right) of Barrack Creek and reaches the bushline after 2$\frac{1}{2}$ hours. From here a long ridge can be followed up to the summit of Goat Hill, presenting little problem in good conditions.

Mt Barron Track: 5 hours return, Grade 2–4.

This track leads up to the bushline below Mt Barron and leaves SH 73 between Goat Creek and the Otira Road Bridge. It climbs steeply for 2$\frac{1}{2}$ hours up through the forest to a trig that dates from the surveying of the Otira Tunnel. The more energetic can continue up through tussock and scrub above the trig, though there is no track.

Cockayne Nature Walk: 40 minutes return, Grade 1.

A short side-road off SH 73 at Kelly's Creek below Otira leads to the start of the Cockayne Nature Walk. This walk commemorates the work of one of New Zealand's great ecologists, Dr Leonard Cockayne, and winds through the podocarp forest near the site of his old cottage at Kelly's Creek.

Hunt's Saddle Track: 7–8 hours return, Grade 2.

The open tussock and bogs atop Hunt's Saddle can be reached on a marked track that is picked up on the true left of Kelly's Creek, up from the Kelly's Creek Shelter off SH 73. The track stays on the true left all the way to the saddle, climbing at one point to avoid a gorge.

Tramping trip summary

The following summary outlines many of the recognised tramping trips in Arthur's Pass National Park. Used with the route descriptions that follow, it can provide a basis for planning a tramp. Remember, however, that these are only suggestions and by using a map and consulting DOC staff many variations on these tramps can be found. The times given make no allowance for delays caused by bad weather.

- Beginning at Klondyke Corner, up Waimakariri Valley to Carrington Hut and/or Waimakariri Falls Hut and return (2–3 days).
- 'Three Pass Trip' beginning at Klondyke Corner, up Waimakariri Valley, over Harman and Whitehorn Pass to Wilberforce Valley, over Browning Pass and Styx Saddle, down Styx Valley to Lake Kaniere–Kokatahi Road (4 days).
- Beginning at Klondyke Corner, up Waimakariri Valley over Harman Pass, down Taipo Valley, over Kelly Range to SH 73 below Otira (4 days).
- Beginning at Klondyke Corner, up Waimakariri Valley, over Waimakariri Col, down Rolleston Valley to SH 73 above Otira (2–3 days).
- Beginning at Arthur's Pass township, over Avalanche Peak to Crow Valley, out to Klondyke Corner via Waimakariri Valley (2 days).
- Beginning from SH 73 southeast of Arthur's Pass township, up Mingha Valley, over Goat Pass and down Deception River to Otira (2 days).
- Beginning on SH 73 below Arthur's Pass, over Temple Col to Goat Pass, and down either Deception or Mingha Valleys to SH 73 (2 days).
- Beginning at SH 73 at Kelly Shelter to Carroll Hut, Kelly Range and return (1–2 days).
- Beginning at SH 73 at Aickens to Lake Kaurapataka and return (2 days).
- Beginning on SH 73 southeast of Arthur's Pass township up Edwards Valley and return (2 days).
- Beginning on SH 73 southeast of Arthur's Pass township, up Edwards Valley and down Hawdon Valley via Tarn Col and Walker Pass (3 days).
- Beginning on SH 73 southeast of Arthur's Pass township, up Edwards Valley, over Turuahuna Pass, down Otehake Valley, and down Taramakau Valley via Lake Kaurapataka to SH 73 at Aickens (4 days).

- Beginning at Hawdon Shelter, up Hawdon Valley and return (2 days).
- Beginning at Andrews Shelter, up Andrews Stream and down Casey Stream, up Poulter Valley to Lake Minchin and return (4 days). Variation: continue over Minchin Saddle and down Taramakau Valley to SH 73 at Aickens (4 days).
- Beginning at Andrews Shelter, up Andrews Stream and down Casey Stream, down Poulter Valley and over Binser Saddle to Andrews Shelter (3 days).

Tramping

THE WAIMAKARIRI RIVER

The grand sweep of the Waimakariri River greets the traveller who enters Arthur's Pass National Park from the east. The river valley itself, and routes over into other catchments, offer a superb range of tramping.

State Highway 73 (640 m) to Carrington Hut (820 m), via Waimakariri River: 4–6 hours, Grade 2–3.

The route to Carrington Hut leads up the Waimakariri Valley, and as much of it is in the braided bed of the river the Waimakariri must be easily fordable, which in normal conditions it usually is. If there is any doubt, however, this route should not be attempted. Begin at the end of the gravel road that leaves SH 73 opposite the shelter at Klondyke Corner. There is no marked track and the route simply crosses the river where necessary and follows the riverbed and flats all the way to Carrington Hut. Generally the quickest and easiest route follows the true left bank to the Crow River, then takes the most direct line, crossing and recrossing the river to Greenlaw Creek. Follow the flats on the true right to Harper Creek, and then the riverbed to the forested corner at the White River junction. Carrington Hut (DOC, 36 bunks, wood stove, radio) is 5 minutes up the White River via a track on the true right, about 4 hours' walk from the road.

As an alternative to beginning from Klondyke Corner, there is also a track which begins at the southern end of the road bridge over the Waimakariri on SH 73. This crosses bluffs above the river and leads to a poled route over Turkey Flat. On the far side the bush edge leads to Anti-Crow Hut (DOC, 6 bunks, open fire). Beyond here follow the main riverbed, as described above. Trampers should note that the Greenlaw Hut marked on some maps has now been removed. Note that there are no bridges over any side-creeks of the Waimakariri. The best fords are generally closer to the main river, but if these creeks are high do not attempt to cross them.

Carrington Hut (820 m) to Waimakariri Falls Hut (1280 m): 3–5 hours, Grade 2–3.

To reach the track to the Waimakariri Falls Hut cross the White River in front of Carrington Hut and follow the true right bank of the Waimakariri to pick up an obvious track. The route stays on the true right to the Waimakariri Falls, where a marked track climbs steeply above the falls and heads upriver crossing the river above the second falls to reach the Waimakariri Falls Hut (DOC, 6 bunks, no cooking or heating facilities) up a tussocky slope overlooking the river.

Waimakariri Falls Hut (1280 m) to Rolleston River (460 m) and SH 73, via Waimakariri Col (1750 m): 7–9 hours, Grade 3–4.

This crossing is primarily a summer route suitable only for experienced parties. It traverses rugged, inspiring country, with rough travelling in the upper Rolleston River, and is a route that is often exposed to avalanche danger until early summer. From the hut follow the true left of the river to the base of obvious bluffs blocking the valley. A scree slope on the true right leads up towards the bluffs and gives access to a hidden but easy line up to the valley beyond. Despite being marked as the crossing on the map, Waimakariri Col is not in fact the easiest route across the Main Divide, as there is a more gentle saddle along the ridge to the west.

To reach the crossing sidle to the west from about 90 m below the main ridge at the head of the valley until an obvious flat saddle, graced with a tarn in summer, is reached. From this saddle drop to and follow the stream draining the glacier underneath Mt Armstrong. When the stream begins to level out veer off on the true left, eventually reaching a shoulder where the lower gorge is visible. Here drop down towards the gorge and begin descending the steep slopes between bluffs to the west and the true left of the gorged stream below. At the northern end of this slope descend down a scree to its left bottom corner and then down to the Rolleston River. Two hundred metres downstream in the riverbed cairns mark the beginning of a track on the true right, about 2½ hours from the col. A marked track leads through bush and scree on the true right, dropping back into the riverbed after some time. The route remains on the true right in the riverbed, with short tracks in the bush bypassing some obstacles. The last climb around bluffs before the railbridge can be avoided when the river is fordable by crossing and staying in the riverbed out to the road.

THREE PASS TRIP

Though much of the Three Pass Trip is not within Arthur's Pass National Park it is often thought of as an Arthur's Pass trip. It involves three crossings of the

Main Divide and gives a magnificent insight into the country on the east and west of the divide. This trip requires tramping experience and good conditions. In winter conditions it is only for the experienced and well-equipped.

Carrington Hut (820 m) to Park Morpeth Hut (880 m) via Harman Pass (1330 m) and Whitehorn Pass (1740 m): 9 hours, Grade 2–4.

Above Carrington Hut (see p. 102) follow the track up the true right of the White River to a crossing and up the unmarked route in the Taipoiti River. Turn at the last low waterfall above the gorge on the true left and follow a worn path from the Taipoiti up to a cairn marking Harman Pass, about 2 hours from Carrington Hut. When descending to the White River from the pass it is worth taking some care to follow this path — if the route is snow-covered bear east across two gullies before dropping down the third gully to the river. To reach Whitehorn Pass from Harman Pass follow south up the ridge from the cairn for 5 minutes before heading off up the valley behind Ariels Tarn.

In clear conditions Whitehorn Pass is very obvious and the approach up the valley from the east is straightforward, about 2 hours' walking from Harmans Pass. The western side of the Whitehorn Pass is steep and unless you have alpine equipment it should not be attempted when snow-covered. The route to Cronin Stream is obvious, leading down through bluffs on scree and rock to the streambed. Care should be taken to avoid falling ice from the Cronin Icefall to the north. The terrain remains rugged in the Cronin Stream, with the best route on the true left until the stream turns a slight corner, where a crossing should be made onto the true right. Just before the stream drops into a gorge, a sporadically marked track starts up from the river on the true right, and leads down through scrub to Park Morpeth Hut (Canterbury Mountaineering Club, 6 bunks, open fire, radio) at the Wilberforce/Cronin stream junction.

Park Morpeth Hut (880 m) to Harman Creek Hut (850 m) via Browning Pass (1410 m): 5 hours, Grade 2–3.

To reach the base of Browning Pass keep in the true left of the Wilberforce riverbed as far as the Clough Memorial. Here ford the river and pick up the track up to the pass. Follow the zigzags up to the fifth (final) 'zig' and climb up the left side of a steep, narrow scree to Browning Pass. This climb should be treated with caution and should not be attempted in snow without adequate experience and equipment. In contrast to the southern side, the Westland side of the pass is a gentle basin which holds Lake Browning and offers, in fine weather, a good campsite. From the pass a track leads past the lake and drops down to cross the Arahura River. Care should be taken to keep to the track, which after crossing the river sidles downstream on the true right until it rejoins the river. Recent maps show a track from this point on the true left but this is now impassable. Instead keep in the true left on the Arahura riverbed until about 400 m above Harman Creek Hut, where an open, rocky creekbed coming in from the true left is climbed for about 100 m to pick up a marked track to Harman Creek Hut (DOC, 6 bunks, open fire).

Harman Creek Hut to Lake Kaniere-Kokatahi Road (90 m) via Grassy Flat Hut (520 m): 7–9 hours, Grade 2–3.

The track as far as Grassy Flat Hut is generally well benched and easy to follow. A little over an hour below Harman Creek Hut the track to Styx Saddle branches off, following stakes over this gentle saddle into forest on the far side. The track emerges on an open flat lower down, and a good ford across the Styx River 5 minutes downstream gives access to the Grassy Flat Hut (DOC, 8 bunks, open fire). Below Grassy Flat Hut recross the Styx River onto the true right bank. The track condition below here is erratic with no track in places and the riverbed providing the only route. It takes around $4^1/_2$ hours, all on the true right, to reach the road, some 14 km from Kokatahi, and a further 15 km from SH 6.

WAIMAKARIRI VALLEY, TAIPO VALLEY AND THE KELLY RANGE

This trip links the Waimakariri and Otira Rivers with a fine route across two passes and through two bushclad valleys. The crossings are suitable for parties with tramping experience and require good conditions.

Carrington Hut (820 m) to Julia Hut (610 m), Taipo River, via Harman Pass (1330 m): 7 hours, Grade 3–4.

For the route to Carrington Hut and to Harman Pass see pages 101–104. From Harman Pass carefully pick a route down through the bluffs to reach the branch of Mary Creek that drains Whitehorn Pass. Cross this stream to reach a terrace above some low bluffs and follow this around until a route all the way down is clearly visible. Back in Mary Creek pick up a marked track on the true left at the bushline. This track leads downriver to reach a swingbridge spanning Mary Creek and the new Julia Hut (DOC, 6 bunks, wood stove) and the older Julia Hut (DOC, 4 bunks, open fire) on the opposite bank, around 3 hours from the pass.

Julia Hut (610 m) to Seven Mile Creek Hut (270 m): 6 hours, Grade 2–3.

Below Julia Hut there is easy walking down to a bridge spanning the Taipo River, where the route crosses and continues downstream on the true left for 20 minutes to the Mid Taipo Hut (DOC, 6 bunks, open fire). From this hut stay on the river flats all the way to a ford upstream of Scotty Creek, except for one point where the flats are connected by a track in the bush. Cross the Taipo to the true right bank and follow the river flats all the way to the older Seven

Mile Hut (DOC, 6 bunks, open fire) 5 minutes past Seven Mile Creek. This can be difficult to cross when in flood.

Seven Mile Creek Hut (270 m) to Kelly Shelter (360 m), via Kelly Range (1370 m) and Carroll Hut (1100 m): 6 hours, Grade 2–4.
The track to the bushline begins about 20 minutes up Seven Mile Creek on the true left where the way becomes blocked on that side. A marked track begins here and leads up to the snow tussock. Once in the tussock follow the more northern of the two ridges to some large tarns. From here climb onto the main ridge of the Kelly Range and follow poles on this ridge north, dropping off it only when above the Carroll Hut (DOC, 8 bunks approx, no cooking or heating facilities) in the tussock basin east of Kelly Saddle. From Carroll Hut an obvious track leads off and down through the bush to the Kelly Shelter and SH 73, 1¹/₂ hours below. Note: When travelling from Carroll Hut to Seven Mile Creek care should be taken to find and follow the track leading down from the bushline on the Kelly Range to the Taipo River.

MINGHA AND DECEPTION VALLEYS
The trip between the Mingha and Deception Valleys is a popular tramp from beech forest to the rainforest of the West Coast. The Main Divide crossing is straightforward and within the capabilities of most trampers.

State Highway 73 (700 m) to Goat Pass Hut (1070 m) via Mingha River: 5–6 hours, Grade 2–3.
From SH 73, 5 km southeast of Arthur's Pass township, this tramp begins by crossing the Bealey River and relies on the Bealey being fordable. Follow up the Mingha, initially on the true right but crossing the river where necessary, to the beginning of the gorge. Here a marked track leaves the river on the true right, avoiding the gorge and rejoining the river after 2 hours. Just beyond this point is the old Mingha Bivvy (DOC, 2 bunks, open fire). The route from here is unmarked and follows the streambed until the main branch of the Mingha swings around towards Temple Col. Here a track leads up the true left of the stream draining Goat Pass, and crosses the pass to Goat Pass Hut (DOC, 20 bunks, radio) just north of the summit. A good side-trip can be made from Goat Pass by climbing up to the east and following the ridge to Lake Mavis.

Goat Pass Hut (1070 m) to SH 73 at Otira (310 m), via the Deception River: 6–7 hours, Grade 3.
This route is principally in the bed of the Deception River, and if the river is high it becomes either very difficult or impossible. From Goat Pass Hut a marked track leads down into the Upper Deception River, where the unmarked route stays either in the riverbed or in the forest on the bank, all the way to the Otira River. The Upper Deception Hut (DOC, 6 bunks, open fire) is about 1

hour from Goat Pass Hut on the true right. Just downstream of where the Deception River flows into the Otira River the Morrison Footbridge spans the Otira to link up with SH 73.

Temple Basin carpark (880 m), SH 73, to Goat Pass Hut (1070 m) via Temple Col (1750 m): 5¹/₂ hours, Grade 1–4.

Temple Col provides a scenic and accessible route to the Mingha and Goat Pass. It requires alpine experience and clear visibility, and is subject to avalanche danger on the Mingha side of Temple Col when under snow. For the route to Temple Col see page 98. From Temple Col pick a route carefully down through the first line of bluffs to the top of the second, where the left hand of two ridges leads down through these bluffs to the streambed. After about 15 minutes in the streambed begin a sidle through scrub on the true left, keeping between the river and bluffs to reach a shoulder. Here the route swings north and continues to the top of Goat Pass. Goat Pass Hut (DOC, 20 bunks, radio) is just to the north of the summit.

AVALANCHE PEAK AND THE CROW VALLEY

This trip traverses a peak above Arthur's Pass township and drops into the valley on the other side, giving a good feel for both the tops and the valleys east of the Main Divide. It requires some alpine tramping experience and should not be attempted in bad weather or winter conditions.

Arthur's Pass township (730 m) to Crow Hut (1040 m) via Avalanche Peak (1750 m): 4–6 hours, Grade 2–4.

For a description of the route to the summit of Avalanche Peak see page 97. From the peak follow the summit ridge west towards the lower peak to reach a saddle on this ridge. From here head towards a stake on the ridge leading north to Mt Rolleston. Follow this ridge for about 30 minutes to an obvious saddle marked with another stake. Here, descend a long scree slope to the Crow River. Do not drop off the ridge until the entire length of this scree is clearly visible. Once in the valley floor follow the riverbed down to Crow Hut (DOC, 12 bunks, open fire) at the bushline on the true right. If travelling the reverse direction from Crow Hut up to Avalanche Peak do not attempt any short cuts across McGrath's Basin; this can be dangerous and difficult.

Crow Hut (1040 m) to Klondyke Corner (640 m), SH 73, via Crow River and Waimakariri River: 4 hours, Grade 2–3.

Below the Crow Hut the track stays on the true right of the Crow River until just above the last creek flowing into the Crow from Mt Bealey on the opposite (true left) bank. Here, ford the river and pick up an unmarked route that cuts through a tongue of beech forest to the grassy flats alongside the Waimakariri. From here to Klondyke Corner there is easy travelling on the true

Arthur's Pass National Park

left, using some worn paths through the bush to avoid the river where it cuts into the bank.

THE EDWARDS AND OTEHAKE VALLEYS

The Edwards and Otehake Rivers share a common pass at their heads, and flow out from the Main Divide in different directions. The Edwards is more easily visited though it is often linked with the more difficult Otehake to form a round trip.

State Highway 73 (700 m) to Edwards Hut (1070 m): 4–5 hours, Grade 2–3.

From SH 73, 5 km south of Arthur's Pass township, this tramp begins by crossing first the Bealey River above its junction with the Mingha River, and then the Mingha River to reach forest on the southern side of the Edwards River near its confluence with the Mingha. Here, a marked track through the bush climbs around the lower Edwards Gorge (which is negotiable if the river is low) and drops back to the river. From here, follow up the true left of the riverbed to the banks of the east branch of the Edwards. Cross the east branch and pick up a marked track on the far bank which leads up the valley above the west branch, eventually emerging on tussock-covered river flats, about 20 minutes below the Edwards Hut (DOC, 16 bunks, wood stove for heating, radio).

Edwards Hut (1070 m) to Otehake Hut (640 m) via Taruahuna Pass (1270 m): 5 hours, Grade 2–4.

Above Edwards Hut an unmarked but easy track follows up the true left of the river to Taruahuna Pass, a huge pile of gravel and broken rock that slid off Falling Mountain in the 1929 earthquake. Cross the pass and head towards the slope leading up to Tarn Col before dropping into the beginnings of the Otehake River. Follow the streambed until it begins to drop away steeply, and then climb onto terraces on the true left. Follow these down, in the bush where necessary, until the riverbed is rejoined where the first major side-creek flows into the Otehake. After crossing this side-creek keep to the true left of the riverbed for about 15 minutes to pick up a marked track which continues down on the true left to reach the Otehake Hut (DOC, 6 bunks, open fire) after 30 minutes.

Otehake Hut (640 m) to Lake Kaurapataka (410 m): 7–8 hours, Grade 3–4.

The tramp down the Otehake is slow and rugged and is suitable only for fit, experienced parties. Although this is to change, the Otehake has been designated a wilderness area for some years, and the tracks have not been maintained. Though the Otehake is never crossed, a side-stream, Whaiti Stream, is, and is often too high to be forded. Also, at one point the Otehake River has to be entered to wade around a bluff. There are no huts in the lower river so a tent should be carried unless SH 73, or huts up the Taramakau River, can be reached by very fast parties.

From the Otehake Hut a marked but very rough track begins, staying high above the gorged river until after 4 hours it drops down to the Otehake to cross Whaiti Stream. Take care to keep to the markers. Below Whaiti Stream the track begins again, climbing for $1^1/_2$ hours before descending back to the river opposite an island in the riverbed. There are campsites on the island and just downstream on the true left. Below the island stay beside or in the true left of the riverbed, until a bluff blocks the way. Here, enter the Otehake to round the bluff and pick up a marked track which leads downstream to where the track to Lake Kaurapataka leaves the river on the true left, a good 7 hours from the hut. This piece of track can be missed if the river is low by keeping in the riverbed, an easier and quicker option in these conditions. (Note that the footbridge over the Otehake River above this junction no longer exists.) From the Otehake the track to Lake Kaurapataka climbs for about 15 minutes to the lake and then follows around its southern side, reaching some pleasant campsites towards the far end. For the route to Aickens see page 109. Note: It is possible to continue on down the Otehake River below the Lake Kaurapataka track junction staying in the riverbed where possible, or in the bush on the true right, to reach the Taramakau River, about 1 hour's walking.

THE TARAMAKAU VALLEY

The Taramakau Valley runs along the northern boundary of the park and is unusually broad for a West Coast valley. The river flats give easy walking, and the major problem likely to be encountered is the flood-prone river and tributaries. The route guides below are for travel down the valley to fit with trips that cross the alps from the east and come down the Otehake via Lake Kaurapataka (above) and Townsend Creek from Lake Minchin (see p. 111).

Lake Kaurapataka (410 m) to State Highway 73 at Aickens (300 m): 3–4 hours, Grade 2–3.

An easy track leaves the western end of Lake Kaurapataka and descends to Pfeifer Creek, where the track continues down on the true right to reach the Taramakau River. Here, easy travel on grassy flats on the true left of the Taramakau leads to a track marked with stakes that cuts through to the bank of the Otira River. To reach Aickens from here, ford the Otira River and pick up a track heading through a gap in the trees to SH 73, and the DOC Aickens Base (which is now locked). If the river is not safely fordable a flood track leads up the true right bank of the Otira River to the Morrison Footbridge, which spans the river to reach SH 73 up from Aickens, adding about 2 hours onto the journey.

Townsend Creek (400 m), Taramakau River to State Highway 73 at Aickens (300 m): 5–6 hours from Locke Stream Hut, 2–4 hours from Kiwi Hut, Grade 2–3.

From the junction of Townsend Creek and the Taramakau, two huts can be easily reached. One hour upstream on the true left at Locke Stream is the Locke Stream Hut (DOC, 18 bunks, wood stove, radio). One hour downstream on the true right of the Taramakau is Kiwi Hut (DOC, 6 bunks, open fire) set back from the river on a terrace above a clearing. If the Taramakau is easily fordable, travel is easy, linking grassy flats with fords in the river. Generally the true right is the easier bank as far as Pfeifer Creek, and below Pfeifer Creek the flats on the true left lead to a marked track that cuts through to the banks of the Otira River. See page 108 for route to Aickens and SH 73.

HAWDON VALLEY

The Hawdon is a picturesque, mostly gentle valley running down from the eastern side of the alps. The tramping is easy and by using some straightforward passes at its head the Edwards can be linked with the Hawdon Valley for a fine trip.

Edwards Hut (1070 m) to Hawdon Hut (760 m) via Taruahuna Pass (1270 m), Tarn Col (1380 m) and Walker Pass (1110 m): 6–9 hours, Grade 3–4.

Taruahuna Pass, Tarn Col and Walker Pass are all, in good summer conditions, suitable for trampers with average experience. For the route to Edwards Hut see page 107. Above Edwards Hut an unmarked but easy track follows up the true left of the river to Taruahuna Pass. To reach Tarn Col, the obvious saddle just north of Falling Mountain, climb the steep slope from the eastern side of the debris atop Taruahuna Pass, following the creek draining the col. When coming down on this side of Tarn Col, a scree slope on the southern end of the col gives a good descent. From the top of the col immediately follow the creek draining the tarn, staying in the creekbed down to the junction with the east branch of the Otehake. Here turn and follow this streambed up towards Walker Pass, where a cairn on the true right marks a patchy track up through scrub to Walker Pass. From the pass follow the creek that drains the tarn on the pass, in places following an unmarked trail. A track begins lower down, marked by a stake on the true left below some rounded cliffs. This leads up to the bush edge and a track which bypasses Twin Falls, emerging in the streambed just up from the Hawdon River. Hawdon Hut (DOC, 16 bunks, radio) is about 20 minutes' travel downstream in the true right of the Hawdon riverbed.

Hawdon Hut to Hawdon Shelter (580 m): 3 hours, Grade 2–3.

Below the hut follow a marked track on the true right downstream to emerge on flats below the East Hawdon Stream junction. If the river is low the best route from here to the Hawdon Shelter lies on the grassy river flats, crisscrossing the river to pick the easiest terrain. If the river is high but fordable, follow the true right until just above Sudden Valley Stream, where the Hawdon should be crossed to reach the shelter.

ANDREWS STREAM AND THE POULTER VALLEY

The country around the Andrews Stream and the broad Poulter River offers a delightful variety of tramping to the east of the divide. Relaxed tramps can be had by staying on the east coast, and for the more adventurous a crossing into the Taramakau offers more challenge.

Andrews Shelter (580 m) to Casey Hut (610 m) via Casey Saddle (780 m): 7 hours, Grade 2–3.

From the Andrews Shelter an undulating track above the true left of this enclosed and forested river valley leads to Hallelujah Flat, about 2¹/₂ hours' walking. An unmarked route continues up these grassy flats past the Hallelujah Bivvy (DOC, 2 bunks, open fire) and over Casey Saddle (which has no obvious summit), keeping on the terrace above the true right of Surprise Stream. At the end of the swampy section of the stream drop into and stay in the streambed for about 15 minutes until a marked track is picked up on the true right. The track leads high above Casey Stream before descending down to the flats and Casey Hut (DOC, 16 bunks, wood stove, radio). Note: When the rivers are running low, the beds of the Andrews, Surprise and Casey Streams can be used as an alternative to the track by those seeking a more adventurous route.

Casey Hut (610 m) to Minchin Bivvy (910 m) via Lake Minchin (760 m): 5¹/₂ hours, Grade 2–3.

From Casey Hut follow an old track, fording Casey Stream out from the hut and crossing a low ridge before reaching the open grassy flats, typical of the Poulter, that lead to the Trust-Poulter Hut (APNP, 6 bunks, open fire). Beyond this hut the track fades out, and once around the corner the route heads in a diagonal line across the Poulter River to the flats on the true left about 500 m below Minchin Stream. Here pick up stakes which lead through scrub to the start of the track to Lake Minchin, an easy and well-marked walk. There are campsites at various places around the picturesque Lake Minchin, and on the flat at its head. At the head of Lake Minchin follow up the river flats and pick up a track on the true right, down from where the river obviously gorges. This unmarked but reasonably obvious route climbs high above the gorge and drops steeply down to Minchin Stream, 5 minutes below its junction with Linwood Stream. Stay in the streambed, crisscrossing the stream up to the Minchin

Bivvy (DOC, 2 bunks, no heating or cooking facilities), easily seen between a fork in the stream.

Minchin Bivvy to Taramakau River (400 m) via Minchin Pass (1080 m) and Townsend Creek: 4–5 hours, Grade 3–4.

Above the bivvy a trail leads through scrub to the slopes below the obvious Minchin Pass. The descent to the Taramakau from Minchin Pass is suitable only for those with fitness and experience, and is impassable if Townsend Creek is high. From Minchin Pass drop down the low ridge on the western side of the pass to the bed of Townsend Creek. Here a very rough 'bush-bash' on terraces just above the true left of Townsend Creek gives the best descent to the more open streambed lower down. The route continues down the rugged bed of Townsend Creek and through a steep gorge to emerge on the riverbed just up from the Taramakau River (see p. 109). Parties climbing in the other direction up Townsend Creek may have difficulty finding the creek that leads to Minchin Pass. The easiest way is to find the junction where three creeks meet — the smaller creek in the middle of this junction is Townsend Creek.

BINSER SADDLE

The loop trip which uses Binser Saddle to cross back out of the Poulter is one of the easiest tramps in the park, with a low pass and no major river crossings. As it is east of the Main Divide the chance of fine weather is also higher.

Casey Hut (610 m) to Pete Stream (550 m) via the Poulter River: 4–5 hours, Grade 2.

From Casey Hut (see p. 110) briefly head down the true right of Casey Stream to pick up an old vehicle track heading downstream on the true right of the Poulter River. This track leads all the way to Pete Stream, for most of the way an easy and open walk in this wide river valley. There are good campsites around Pete Stream.

Pete Stream (550 m) to Andrews Shelter (580 m) via Binser Saddle (1110 m): 4 hours, Grade 2.

On the true right of Pete Stream pick up a track on the edge of the terrace leading into the bush and winding up to Binser Saddle, a crossing which remains in forest. Travel on the western side of Binser Saddle is straightforward, emerging on flats alongside the Waimakariri River just east of Lower Farm Stream. The Andrews Shelter is about 30 minutes' walking from this point.

OTHER ROUTES

Other lesser-used routes in Arthur's Pass include trips up the Sudden Valley Stream, up the East Branch of the Hawdon, up into the headwaters of the

Poulter River, and the Thompson Stream. On the southern side of the Taramakau a track climbs up above the bushline to the Townsend Hut, and a reasonably popular route leads over Harpers Pass at the head of the Taramakau out of the national park into Lake Summer Forest Park — there is a pamphlet available at park headquarters which describes this walk.

index